The World's Disappearing Wildlife

Dr. Maurice Burton
Robert Burton

Also published as a supplement
to the International Wildlife Encyclopedia.

ARCO PUBLISHING COMPANY, INC.
New York

CONTENTS

A grey seal, well camouflaged on this beach

*page 2:
A leopard in
a relaxed mood*

Editor Liz Glaze

Published 1978 by Arco Publishing Company, Inc.,
219 Park Avenue South, New York, N.Y. 10003

© Marshall Cavendish Corporation 1978

Also published as a supplement to
The International Wildlife Encyclopedia

Library of Congress Catalog Card Number 78-55728

ISBN 0-668-04668-6

Printed in United States of America

INTRODUCTION

This book is intended to give an up-to-date review of the situation of world wildlife and the major changes that have taken place during the 1970s. Inevitably the emphasis must be on conservation, since it affects the world's fauna, and in this field we shall be examining the gains and losses of recent years. We shall also be taking note of significant increases in knowledge of selected species, of their behaviour and other aspects of their biology. These two aspects of natural history are closely linked, for often the best conservation is dependent on more detailed information on what an animal does, how it lives and on what makes it tick.

Overshadowing all else in the massive global effort to stem the damaging influences on the world's fauna are the demands made by the accelerating increases in human populations and the strains these impose on limited natural resources. Suddenly mankind has become aware that the world has an energy crisis on its hands and that unless he can realize his optimistic hopes and solve, or at least mitigate, this crisis by the use of solar energy, the effect on the world's living resources may well be disastrous.

In the meantime, the menace to the world's animals remains. The destruction or spoliation of the habitat and the often wanton killing of a wide variety of animals, not merely for food but more especially for their skins and other parts—such as elephant tusks—has been devastating and has happened frequently for no better reason than to satisfy the whims of fashion or ignorant superstition.

These are the broad considerations and they can be best appreciated with reference to the smaller details of conservation efforts. A single example of the conflicting elements within a relatively small area is seen in Morocco, the country, which with Tunisia, Algeria and Libya constitutes the Mediterranean fringe of the arid northern half of Africa. Helped by French scientists, the Moroccan government did two things. They drew up a list of birds and animals needing protection and distributed posters portraying them to forest stations throughout the country. The forestry department were given sole responsibility for the nation's wildlife. The

Below left: reaching up to find fresh food, the African elephant

Below right: a clawless otter demonstrating its powerful paws

stimulus for this action arose from a visit by the president of the World Wildlife Fund a few years previously, but unfortunately there was no follow-up and with these initial steps conservation, in a practical sense, came to an end.

The official in charge of the campaign was, unsuitably, an engineer and the forestry department in his charge saw the economic advantage of quick-growing pines, so plantations were consequently developed into the usual sterile stands of trees with an increasingly acid topsoil. The rich Forêt Diplomatique, near Tangier, was cleared of its undergrowth for the supposed benefit of tourists and, worse still, the clearing was carried out in spring when bird-nesting was in full swing, instead of delaying it until the eggs had hatched and the young had flown.

Governments, from their various capitals, may enact game laws, but such legislation is useless unless it gains the support of the rural people who are on the spot. The mistakes made did nothing to encourage the people living in the countryside, for whom the business of living is hard. It is a similar story in many other parts of the world where the need for conservation is equally urgent. In Morocco, for example, the local people persisted in raiding the established deciduous forests for firewood, building materials and wood for charcoal burning, despite restrictive laws. Again, birds of all kinds suffered from loss of the undergrowth, as well as through the traditional raiding of nests, trapping and shooting for food and to satisfy local superstitions. Heads of brightly coloured birds, for example, are nailed to the walls of homes for good luck.

It would be wholly unjustified to point the accusing finger at Morocco or at any other developing country needing to assert itself in a modern world. The mistakes made there have all been made before. The Moroccan example is described here to illustrate the kinds of conflicting interests, such as the need for wise forestry and the call for quick returns in the form of marketable lumber, and the need for preserving undergrowth against the short-term, but locally urgent, requirements of firewood and charcoal. At least Morocco has made a start in the right direction.

The concept of conservation is not a new one, it has been put into practice wherever and whenever wise husbandry has been the rule. As applied to animals, conservation was first deliberately pursued centuries

Below left: America's friendly and cheerful bluebird

Below right: an iguana basking in the sun

ago in India. What is new is that the matter has become one for urgent consideration by mankind and this is now appreciated in all but the poorest and most underdeveloped areas of the world. This urgency has, however, only recently been recognized and we are still learning, sometimes by our mistakes, about the preservation of species threatened with extinction.

The best chance of success is to create a reserve around a surviving wild population. Otherwise it might be necessary to transfer the survivors to a reserve in another area within the species' natural range, or to one elsewhere in the world where the ecological conditions closely approximate those of the natural habitat. The last of these three options has been used for the Arabian oryx and the aye-aye, and in considering the oryx it could reasonably be asked whether the enormous trouble and expense is justifiable.

To finance the expedition to capture the three remaining Arabian oryxes, help came from six governments, five zoos, scores of societies and clubs, hundreds of private individuals and several commercial concerns. These included various oil companies, and an electricity company in Kenya which 'emptied its showrooms of ovens in order to heat the oryxes' quarantine quarters to save them from the cold'. The greater the number of people contributing to an enterprise the greater, as a rule, is the publicity, and the more bizarre the story unfolded by it, the longer it is remembered. This is one way of getting the message across to those who matter most; those who, for profit or other ignoble reasons, bring danger to wildlife. Inevitably the success of conservation measures depends not so much on the influence of remote governments as on the people living in the area inhabited by the threatened animal.

A striking example of how this can work comes from Melbourne, Australia, in 1977. Glaziers working on a multi-million dollar building refused to install windows until a sister company of the owners of the building agreed to end sand-mining on Fraser Island. There had been controversy over the bad effects of the sand-mining. The owners tried to sell the building to avoid trouble with the glaziers, but they promptly put a ban on another, more vital, property belonging to the owners. Finally the owners agreed to restrict the mining, while the union, the Federated Furnishing Trades Society, lobbied for the island to be made a national

Below left: a bull caribou showing his antlers to advantage on an Alaskan ridge

Below right: well-known for their social structure, the spotted hyaena

park. A few months later it became Australia's first National Estate and mineral exports were banned except under special circumstances.

As in all other activities the best of intentions can be marred by one seemingly trivial event and the progress achieved by the devotion and self-sacrifice of many can be entirely ruined by the self-seeking of one or a few individuals. So the history of conservation is and will remain a desperate mixture of hope and disappointment, progress and impending disaster.

In dividing this book into six sections the first two are devoted to these contrasting aspects of what is now a global effort to halt the slide of our wildlife to total devastation. In the third section we shall be examining the effects of some of the more extravagant human fashions on the fur-bearing animals. These same demands from the almost insatiable craze for novelty in human apparel and appurtenances bear hardly less heavily on the world of reptiles. In this same area we find that there are similar ravages from the ever-growing enthusiasm for pet-keeping as well as the overkill of turtles, for example, for the table. So our fourth section examines what is happening to the reptiles of the world. The fifth section must, of necessity, move into the realm of the harvest of the seas, the decline in the fisheries and the decimation of the great whales and the seals.

In these five sections will recur the insistent note that the success or failure of all conservation depends more than anything else on the acquisition of knowledge. Therefore, the sixth and final section will be devoted to a few of the more striking advances in our knowledge of animals in the 1970s. These can only be a collection of examples, chosen more or less at random, because as each year passes the accumulation of zoological knowledge accelerates. We can only pick and choose from a vast store available. The same, indeed, is true for the previous five sections, so at best, within the limited space available, we can do little more than arrange a few straws to indicate which way the winds are blowing.

Finally, a cautionary note is needed. A study of the literature on conservation leaves the impression that sudden and dramatic changes in the information available all too frequently occur. This is true in all walks of life, but it seems to be especially true in the realm of conservation. There must be warning, therefore, that information given in these pages is that known, or believed to be correct, at the time of going to press.

Below left: an orang-utan, vulnerable to man's incursions into the jungle

Below right: a hatchling green turtle on its hazardous journey to the sea

HOPE FOR DISAPPEARING ANIMALS

Gorilla   Addax   Orang-utan   Arabian oryx
Whooping crane   Flightless teal   Peregrine falcon
Honeycreeper   Woolly monkey   Cahow   Magpie robin
Solenodon   Mauritius kestrel   Marsupial mouse

The story of wildlife conservation tends to make somewhat depressing reading. All too often animals have been hunted and killed ruthlessly, to the point of extinction, without any thought for the consequences. It has been realized, sometimes too late, that future generations will be able to see pictures of the animals, but never a living example and that an exterminated species is lost forever, never to be re-created.

There are, however, several instances where preservation has come just in time and has been successful enough to put the species back on the map of world wildlife.

This first section describes gains represented by both the preservation of some species and by the actual discovery and re-discovery of others.

The mountain gorilla is hardly seen in zoos and is the victim of the destruction, by man, of the forests it lives in and of hunting. The graceful addax has been severely poached by the nomads who share its harsh desert home, and the orang-utan has also been at risk because its jungle habitat has been so drastically reduced. The Arabian oryx became something of a challenge to hunt and the whooping crane has been shot down whilst on its lengthy migration route.

These, as well as many other animals, have been at considerable risk, but some form of action has taken place which has effectively rescued the animal from almost certain extinction.

A troop of mountain gorillas in its typical jungle habitat

Gorilla: *a message of hope and despair*

The mountain gorilla, in common with the pygmy chimpanzee and the orang-utan, is the most endangered of the great apes. The main causes for this are: the actual destruction of the forests in which they live, the interference with their habitat and the fact that they are hunted. The most certain method of bringing about the preservation of all three threatened apes would be to leave strictly alone the areas in which they live. Unfortunately we are living in a changing world, which is in a state of upheaval due to political changes and expanding human populations, with new economic needs that make this preservation difficult to put into action.

Two contrasting habitats

There are three kinds of gorilla: the western lowland or common gorilla (*Gorilla gorilla gorilla*); the eastern lowland gorilla (*G. gorilla graueri*) and the mountain gorilla (*G. gorilla beringei*). The first of these three subspecies is confined to the Zaire river basin. The second lives in lowland forest to the east of the Zaire river. The third, the mountain gorilla, inhabits the Virunga volcanoes and the Mount Kahuzi region, or Kahuzi-Biega, at altitudes of between 9000 and 11,000 feet. Both these last two regions are similar in that they have ground cover of a dense layer of tall herbs, where the gorillas find most of their food, and a rainfall of seventy inches, but whereas the Virunga is bracing, with night temperatures close to freezing, the Kahuzi-Biega forest is hot and humid. In the Virunga there are only two main tree species, up to sixty feet high, and in the Kahuzi-Biega there is a mosaic of some twenty-five species, the largest reaching well over 100 feet.

The Virunga consists of a chain of five extinct volcano peaks straddling the borders of Zaire, Rwanda and Uganda. This means that the first difficulty in planning conservation measures is that three governments need to be persuaded to co-operate for any measures to be fully effective. It was in the Virunga that Dr George Schaller spent two years, in 1959 and 1960, studying the mountain gorillas at first hand. Harold Coolidge, of the United States National Academy of Sciences, had visited central Africa in 1927 and, unable to go again himself, was anxious to launch an expedition to study the gorillas. Schaller was chosen, and his study resulted in the revolution of our ideas about the nature and behaviour of man's nearest relative. The more important consideration for our discussion was that he was able to form an idea of the mountain gorillas' numbers so that they could be compared with later findings.

Schaller had ten groups of gorillas under observation, totalling 169 individuals in the saddle area around Kabara. In 1975 John MacKinnon spent six weeks in Zaire, and of this he spent three days around Kabara, too short a time, as he admits, to make a proper census, but he came to the conclusion that numbers then, fifteen years later, were well below Schaller's figures. Even so his census was based on positive clues. For example, on the northwestern slopes of Karisimbi, where Schaller had found two large groups, the only signs of gorillas were several months old. Yet there was no sign of habitat destruction, so the only conclusion was that the reduction in numbers was the result of increased human activity. There were traces of poaching and dogs, and also of cattle herdsmen, on the saddle at Kabara and on the Karisimbi slopes and the only gorillas they encountered at close range screamed and moved hurriedly away. The late Dr Victor van Straelen, who devoted so much of his life to the maintenance

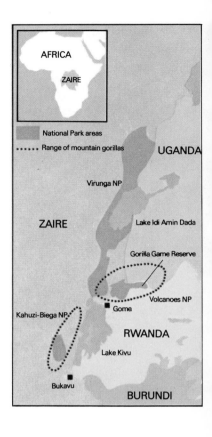

The positions of the Kahuzi-Biega National Park, Zaire, and the Gorilla Game Reserve (on the borders of Uganda, Rwanda and Zaire) in relation to the extent of the range of the mountain gorilla. The small tourist town of Bukavu is near by

of the parks of what was then the Belgian Congo, claimed that he could tell, the moment he entered a park, whether or not poachers had been at work.

Since the Parc National des Virungas is at an altitude of between 7000 and 10,000 feet and consists of dense forest it is surprising that it does not offer greater security for the animal inhabitants. The high altitude would also make any attempt at preservation very difficult. Even so, the Kahuzi-Biega area is, according to MacKinnon, the most promising, in view of the enlargement of the area that was being planned in 1976. He also suggested that there were signs that the Virunga population was suffering from inbreeding and saw, as a remedy, the introduction of new blood into it.

Zoo in the wild

The Kahuzi-Biega Park, 230 miles square, is only twenty-five miles from the tourist town of Bukavu and it was in this part that, in 1966, Adrien DeSchryver started to encourage two gorilla families to become used to the presence of people. His attempts were so successful that since 1972 tourists have been allowed to view the gorillas and can be guaranteed a view of them at about five yards distance. The visits are controlled and escorted by African staff—former hunters—and streams of visitors flow to what is virtually a 'zoo in the wild', comparable with Treetops in East Africa or, at a lesser level, with organized look-out posts (little better than hides) in bird sanctuaries. This principle of 'zoos in the wild' probably has a promising future as a means of sustaining public interest in wildlife as well as encouraging measures for the protection of it.

In the Kahuzi-Biega Park, for example, mountain gorillas were being heavily hunted, the young in particular were being killed off and the remaining adults were becoming aggressive and dangerous. Up to 1970, the year hunting was stopped and the park created, a census showed a total population of about 150 gorillas. A first result of the cessation of hunting was an exceptionally high number of births. The gorillas, also, were quick to recognize that danger from man was a thing of the past.

The benefit from DeSchryver's pioneer work can be contrasted with the almost complete absence of mountain gorillas from any of the world's zoos. This is to be expected because the lowland gorillas are more easily accessible to collectors for zoos, and also because there is little obvious

Adrien De Schryver talks to a male mountain gorilla. He was so successful in his attempts to make gorillas become used to the presence of man that today visitors can see the apes close to in a 'zoo in the wild' and can be guaranteed a view of them at five yards distance

difference between them and only specialists can tell them apart. To the casual visitor to a zoo a gorilla is a gorilla, whether it comes from a mountain, or a lowland habitat. The main outward difference is that the mountain gorilla has long body hair. There is also a marked difference in the region above the nostrils, lowland gorillas having a distinct 'lip' to the nose, overhanging the septum.

Changing trends in thought

To maintain viable populations of the rare mountain gorilla in 'zoos in the wild' requires more detailed knowledge on their habits and physiology than is at present available. This is where the present trend towards breeding gorillas in zoos can be beneficial, not only to the common gorilla but also to the mountain gorilla. In 1967, Professor John Napier, of the Unit of Primatology at the Royal Free Hospital School of Medicine, in London, recorded that there had been eight births, including one pair of twins. The *International Zoo Yearbook* for 1975 was able to record 136 births for the period 1956–1975, of which 105 survived, among the more than 400 gorillas in various zoological collections.

It is not long since it seemed that custodians of zoos were content if their solitary gorilla was on show to visitors in a cage just large enough to give the animal standing room and sufficient space to stretch its arms. These pathetic spectacles were superseded, often under pressure of public opinion, by more roomy cages and then by the addition of a mate. Even then, when a male and a female were brought together, mating did not necessarily take place. And even if it did and a subsequent birth took place the mother could not always be counted on to give proper attention to her offspring. Hand-rearing became necessary, and this, together with other factors, led inevitably to serious and intensive studies of the reproductive biology and post-natal care in gorillas. At the same time it was realized that further importation of animals from the wild could no longer be justified.

Parental affection. Catching baby gorillas for zoos often involved killing not only the mother but other adults who came to her rescue. If birth took place in captivity hand-rearing was often necessary because of lack of interest on the part of the mother

A mountain gorilla pauses to feed while swinging through the trees at Kahuzi-Biega. Rarely seen in zoos because it is less accessible to collectors, it has longer body hair than the lowland gorilla, but usually only experts can spot the difference

It not only meant denuding populations already under menace from other causes but also, as we know from experiences even within the enlightened twentieth century, the catching of them involved unacceptable cruelty. There are stories on record from the first half of this century of collectors having to shoot the mother in order to capture her infant, and perhaps one or more additional females if they came to her aid, as well as the old male, who tried to protect them all.

A centre for breeding gorillas

One venture may perhaps serve as a pilot model for the breeding of gorillas in captivity. This is the gorilla complex in the Jersey Zoo in the Channel Islands, the home of the Wildlife Preservation Trust, under the energetic direction of Gerald Durrell, well known for his books on wild animals. Whether it will ever be practicable to use this and other similar centres for breeding gorillas and then returning them to the wild, as has been the expressed hope of some enthusiasts, remains to be seen. Even if this proved over-optimistic there is still tremendous value in such schemes. If it was attempted to replenish or restore natural populations in suitable habitats in the wild, the success or failure of the scheme would hinge largely on the knowledge gained in such centres. Taking the most gloomy view, the scientific studies made in such centres, combined with the field observations of people like George Schaller, would at least ensure that important zoological knowledge would have been collected from the last survivors of the species. Moreover, this zoological knowledge could serve as a collateral contributing to the rescue of some other species.

The question as to whether a species is endangered or not revolves basically around the numbers still in existence, and this can only be determined by a census. Nations take censuses of their populations periodically by requiring every citizen, on a given day, to fill in a form, the forms then being collected and the numbers counted. This gives an almost precise registration of populations. For wild animals the census must, of necessity, be less precise, even when the census-taking is well organized. Some years ago a census was made of the mallard, or wild duck, in Britain. A vast team of observers was mustered and each was asked to note, on a particular day, the numbers of mallard seen in a particular area, throughout the country. When the census forms were duly sent in to headquarters the results were plotted on a large map marked with a grille and the numbers of mallard determined with moderate accuracy, within a few thousand either way. Despite this organization the map was disappointingly unrepresentative due to gaps for the places in which no volunteers had offered to help.

Counting mountain gorillas

Although there are records, called censuses, of estimated numbers for gorillas, the results are no more than pragmatic. It is always said that the western lowland gorilla is 'common' and estimates of their numbers are based on one or a few observers counting the gorillas seen within a circumscribed area. This is then related as a fraction of the whole range of the typical habitat and by extrapolation the total figure for the whole population is given as 'probably about 90,000 to 100,000'. The range of the eastern lowland gorilla is smaller and the estimate of numbers would probably be more accurate, but it would still be little more than an informed guess of 'between 5000 to 15,000' (in 1959). The mountain gorilla, living in an even more restricted range, has been subject to more careful 'censuses' at different times, by one or a few observers stationing themselves at particular points, getting to know the families of gorillas in the area, then following their trails and, partly by sighting the individual animals and partly by interpreting the signs they leave behind, arriving at a reasonable estimate of numbers. Each gorilla, for example, makes a sleeping nest each night, so a count of fresh nests in a given area on one day gives a fair estimate. Individuals seen moving about can also be recorded in a notebook by their special characteristics, such as sex, size, colour of hair, but more especially by facial characteristics. The last of these is the most reliable, and particularly the shape and markings of their 'noseprints'. The diagram on the right shows the noseprints of several different animals.

Census results

The results of these 'censuses', when collated from the published works of the various authors, are disappointing. Thus, Schaller (1963) estimated the numbers of mountain gorillas in the Virunga Park at 400–500, Fossey (1970) gave 375–400, Groves (1971) gave 'perhaps about 300', Harcourt and Groom (1972) 'fewer than 1000'. Groom (1973) gives no overall total, only precise figures for a few selected areas within the range. All give the impression that the numbers are decreasing and, in the course of their census noted signs of the whittling down of the area of the Park for crop-growing (for example in Rwanda for growing *Pyrethrum* for use in pesticides), cattle-grazing, wood-cutting, bee-keeping, poaching, the piping away of water, erosion, as well as the usual persecution by organized hunting and isolated killings.

The pattern of conservation for all gorillas is therefore a mosaic of hope and despair, especially for the least-numerous subspecies, the mountain gorilla, but with the overlying message of hope that the problem is being exposed, which is the first step towards a solution.

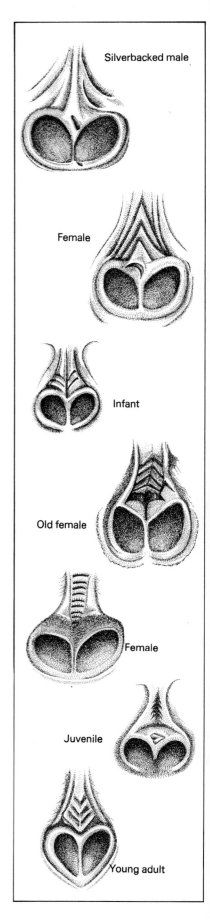

Silverbacked male

Female

Infant

Old female

Female

Juvenile

Young adult

Addax: *desert antelope threatened by desert man*

In the history of mankind it is found that small ethnic groups with a primitive culture tend to retreat, when pressurized by more advanced peoples, into forests and mountains, on to islands and into deserts. Animal species do the same. It comes as no surprise, therefore, that several of the species threatened with extinction have adapted successfully to the rigours

Right: the addax, with graceful curving horns, once much prized by hunters, has distinctive brown patches and a white X over the face

Below: a detail of a frieze from the palace at Nineveh, showing two antelopes

of the desert conditions and have flourished there until man has intervened. Of these the addax, an antelope related to the Arabian oryx, seems to be the most fully equipped for living in areas of large sand dunes and rocky desert, able to subsist on sparse vegetation and very little water. Not the least of its adaptations are its large splayed hoofs, which help it move over the inhospitable ground. Another is its ability to tolerate high temperatures without significant water loss.

The addax, a large antelope with spiral horns up to thirty-six inches long, is white with a grey-brown tinge in summer. In winter, when its coat is a decided grey-brown throughout, it digs shallow holes in the sand with its hoofs for shelter against the wind. Its original range extended over most of the northern half of Africa, from the Atlantic coast to the Nile, from northern Nigeria and Cameroon in the south, to the Mediterranean coast in the north. Today it is largely confined to the Ouadi Rime-Ouadi Achem Reserve in Chad, where it numbers some 800.

Policing against poachers

At the moment the addax is in a precarious situation, but there is hope that something may be done for it that will not only preserve it but make its preservation a practical proposition. Permanent wells have been sunk around the perimeter of the reserve and the nomads, Arab and Gorane herders of camels, goats, sheep and cattle, tend to stay near them for long periods, their herds grazing the vegetation within a thirty-mile radius of each one. This is, in fact, a disadvantage because the nomads have long utilized the addax, as well as the scimitar-horned oryx and the dama gazelle, for meat, especially at the end of the dry season when other food is giving out. So although the reserve has been established for their protection there is still the temptation for the nomads to poach. On the other hand, the concentration of the nomads around the wells makes it easier to police these areas against poachers.

Efficient meat-producer

Nobody can blame the nomads for battening on the addax. Man and antelope are sharing the same harsh habitat and the antelope represents a natural crop that supplements the nomads' domestic herds. The ultimate solution must be so to conserve the addax that it can be used for food on a sustained yield basis. This could be the solution for other large animals that are being pressurized out of existence by man's domestic stocks. An animal adapted to its habitat is a more efficient meat-producer in the Tropics than domesticated cattle, sheep and goats.

Easy to chase

If the account given in 1966 by Hubert Gillet of the Natural History Museum in Paris is a criterion, the addax is a natural prey of the poacher. Its great weakness, according to Gillet, is that it cannot maintain speed for long. Closely pursued in a car at thirty miles per hour it is completely out of breath in eight minutes. Even at twelve miles per hour it is breathless in well under an hour and after any long period it is so exhausted that it can make no effort to go through the motions of defending itself. A hunter on horseback has only to chase the animal at a gentle trot to be sure of catching it within the hour with no further effort.

There is yet another characteristic that militates against the addax. It cannot tolerate the presence of strangers. If disturbed frequently it is apt to move off and travel a long way out of its habitat where it dies from starvation, for the addax feeds mainly on two species of grass and a species of small shrub. Provided it can get both of these plants it can go without drinking for considerable periods of time, but without them it dies from malnutrition.

The addax has magnificent twisting horns, they are displayed here in all their glory and reflected on the animal's splendid white coat. They can grow up to thirty-six inches in length

Orang-utan: *help for orangs, education for people*

The orang-utan, the least known of the four kinds of living apes, is found today in small areas on the islands of Borneo and Sumatra. Subfossil remains, usually of teeth, have been dug up in many places on both islands and have also been found on mainland Asia, as far north as Peking.

It hardly requires a crystal ball to determine how the ape was eliminated from most of eastern Asia. The causes were probably the same as more recent ones, with only slight variations in time and severity.

Piecing together the past

Since the seventeenth century the story has been pieced together of how the local peoples cut down the forests forming the apes' habitat, killing the orangs either for food or out of fear of them, or keeping them as pets, even having a female in the communal long houses for the sexual gratification of the men. Similar activities can be deduced for the earlier inhabitants of eastern Asia, including the Stone Age people, partly by study of orang remains found in archaeological sites and partly by analogy with what the eighteenth- and nineteenth-century explorers and traders found in Sumatra and Borneo. The main difference being that during the Stone Age, a period of pre-history, and succeeding millenia, human populations were more sparse and their depredations had minimal impact on the wildlife of the time.

The reduced and still dwindling populations of orangs then received the full impact of the visiting Europeans, acting either for profit or in the name

A female orang sitting sedately in the fork of a tree, while her two youngsters swing energetically in the upper branches. A way of life sadly denied numerous unfortunate orangs kept in zoos

With a tremendous amount of care an orang is caught in the jungle. It will then be taken to a special rehabilitation centre and released into the wild at a later date in another area

of science. There developed an almost insatiable demand for orang skulls and skins for museums and live specimens for zoos. Young orangs were needed for zoos, research stations, or as pets, which meant killing the mother to capture the juvenile, and sometimes more than one adult if others tried to succour the mother. For every five or so captured and transported overseas, all but one was likely to die *en route*. The survivor soon succumbed under the appalling conditions of the zoos of those times and a replacement would then be needed. Too often orangs were kept in cages so low they could hardly stand, a tragic contrast to their natural way of life, which was to swing by the arms through trees!

The greater menace leading to the dramatic decline in numbers was the behaviour of the local peoples, as described by G. S. de Silva, the game warden for Sabah (formerly British North Borneo). The greater part of Sabah is dense evergreen rain forest, which has been opened up at an accelerated rate during the last two decades. Not only is the habitat of the orangs being reduced in acreage but during jungle-clearing operations female orangs are shot or otherwise killed and their young captured, despite stringent protection laws. There is reason to believe, also, that the apes are hunted in connection with pagan rituals and the making of so-called medicines. Hunting is, however, a way of life for the indigenous people and arguments in favour of conservation, whether on cultural, scientific or aesthetic grounds, are apt to fall on deaf ears and game laws are seen as little more than a constant source of irritation. Nevertheless, all illegal killings or captures that come to the notice of the authorities are investigated, the offenders prosecuted and carcases and live animals confiscated and handed to the Chief Game Warden.

Baby orangs confiscated

There was a similar situation in neighbouring Sarawak and it was Barbara Harrisson, in particular, who brought the sad plight of the remaining orangs to the notice of conservationists. It was largely the result of her efforts that game laws were tightened in Indonesia and Malaysia and international agreements made to control the export and import of live orangs. Baby orangs were intercepted at sea and air ports, confiscated and sent to approved zoos and the traffic in these unfortunate apes was reduced dramatically. Then, in the early 1960s, the indefatigable Barbara conceived the plan of setting up rehabilitation centres. Prior to 1963, all confiscated orangs had been sent to zoos in other parts of the world.

Plan for rehabilitation

Up to this point the decline and attempted rescue followed the now familiar lines of the decline and attempted rescue of so many of the world's threatened species. Barbara Harrisson's plan contained a new element: to rehabilitate the orangs and later release them into the wild, a plan delightful in its simplicity, but one that encountered several snags.

Teaching young orang-utans to be self-sufficient proved to be a difficult task since, like baby humans, so little of their behaviour is instinctive that careful supervision and instruction are needed during their formative years. And knowledge of their behaviour, certainly in the early years of the scheme, was less extensive than that of the biology of other apes. Even so, the Sabah Forest Department was impressed and a large rehabilitation programme was planned, to be centred at Sepilok, near Sandakan. The orangs were transferred there and when a female gave birth to two babies Sepilok was opened up as a tourist attraction.

The problems that have to be met in a rehabilitation centre were vividly set forth by De Silva, in 1970, based on experiences at Sepilok. There were then twenty-two orangs at the centre, of both sexes and ranging from three to thirteen years of age. Most had suffered from improper feeding and were underweight, although a few had lived luxuriously and had been treated more or less like human beings. The majority had been in captivity for varying lengths of time and the longer this time the more closely they resembled domesticated animals, with consequent physiological and psychological changes. They had become subdued and dependent on their

Below: the orangs are fed and cared for

Below right: they become attached to their human guardians, but over-dependency can cause problems when they return to the jungle

Back in the jungle, a self-reliant orang makes his nest

keepers, had acquired new habits and feeding patterns. Some were sick, many were infested with hookworm and roundworm, and all were susceptible to disease, such as malaria, bronchial infections, dysentery, hepatitis and the like. An extreme example of physical degradation was a male that had been confined since infancy in an iron cage five and a half by four and a half by three feet, giving him barely room to move, with bars at two-inch intervals on all sides. He was flat-footed, his fingers could not be flexed owing to atrophy of the muscles, he did not try to walk, but pushed himself along the ground in a squatting position using his hands.

Too much attention given to the ape inmates makes them unwilling to leave the centre. They may become fixated on their keepers, sometimes affectional to the point of jealousy. Autoeroticism may show itself, the product of boredom. Above all, being regularly fed they are apt to make no attempt to find their own food. Once they are in a fit enough physical and mental state to be returned to their natural habitat, this problem is overcome by putting the food out on tables progressively farther into the jungle and then reducing the amount of food.

In the 1970s several observers studied the apes in the wild over an

22

aggregate of tens of thousands of hours. Dr John MacKinnon, who was one of these observers, has reported that one of their important findings was that the density of orang populations is ten times greater than was thought. The animals are frequently overcrowded because the forests are being reduced faster than their numbers are being depleted. Moreover, orangs made homeless become bad-tempered nomads, disrupting the social harmony and breeding success of the rest of the population. To liberate one or two orangs from a rehabilitation centre into such a situation makes only a negligible contribution to total numbers, but could do harm to the population as a whole. In addition, a semi-tame animal, kept for a period of time in a rehabilitation centre has, when released, to learn or be taught the art of living in trees; no simple task for a ground-dwelling human guardian. There is also always the risk that a rehabilitant may carry disease or parasites against which the wild populations have no immunity.

The illicit traffic in orang-utans has now been brought to a low level. The rehabilitation centres have their uses, limited though they are, in restoring their patients to normal. Knowledge of the way of life of the apes is increasing. What is most needed now is wise management of the forests, by which the lumber crop can be extracted without inhibiting the natural regeneration. Meanwhile, it may be possible to develop these rehabilitation centres in order to stock, with 'graduates' from these centres, suitable forest areas elsewhere which contain no orangs.

One of the more important values of the rehabilitation centres lies in their use for educating the local inhabitants to the point where they themselves will want to keep the animals in their forests and protect them rather than just exploiting them ignorantly.

A young orang, at a rehabilitation centre, playing

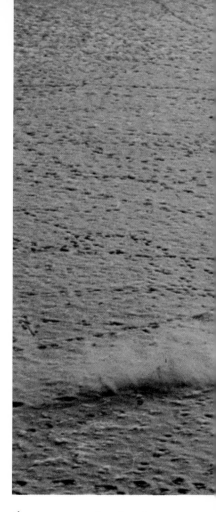

Arabian oryx: *a modern phoenix*

The Arabian oryx probably qualifies as the most beautiful, certainly the most elegant, of the Afro-Asian antelopes. Also known as the Beatrix oryx, it stands forty inches at the shoulder, is almost pure white with chocolate legs and face patches and long, slender, almost straight horns in both sexes. Two centuries ago it ranged over the extensive deserts of southwestern Asia, from Syria and Iraq in the north to the southern border of the Arabian peninsula.

There is a mystique attached to white animals, but the mystique of the Arabian oryx was enhanced by its ability to survive in the most inhospitable deserts, to shelter from the blazing sun where there was seemingly no shade, to go without water indefinitely and to subsist on scattered patches of grass. In this arduous existence it was aided by its speed of foot. So hunting the oryx demanded following its spoor in the sand for days on end and finally killing an animal, which even at close range, blended to near-invisibility against the sun-drenched desert, with only the puffs of sand thrown up by its hoofs to disclose its position. It is not surprising that, for the Arabs, to have killed an oryx was a symbol of virility, of prowess in hunting and of physical endurance. By its vigilance and ability to travel long distances, an oryx might lead a Bedouin hunter on for ten to fourteen days.

An additional touch of mysticism is supplied by the oryx being, it is believed, the origin of the unicorn legend. In both animals the horns were thought to have magical properties and eating the animal's flesh was meant to confer strength and provide a panacea against most ills.

The killing of oryxes as proof of virility made only small inroads into their numbers until the advent of motorized vehicles, automatic weapons and the riches gained from oil. Then Arab nobles, together with British and American executives and technicians helping to exploit the oil reserves, using modern arms, hunted the Arabian oryx almost to extinction.

Steady decrease in numbers

The alarm was raised as a consequence of a survey made by the American, Dr Lee Talbot, in the course of a tour of southern Asia on behalf of the Survival Service Commission of the International Union for Conservation of Nature. He reported that the oryx had been steadily eliminated throughout most of its range by the 1930s, leaving only a remnant of the original number in the Nafud Desert, on the borders of Saudi Arabia and Jordan, and another in the Rub al Khali, in what is now the Yemen. The last fresh spoor had been seen in the Nafud in 1954 and Talbot concluded that the species was extinct except for the few remaining in the Rub al Khali and those in captivity.

Talbot's report was published in the journal of the Fauna Preservation Society, London, appropriately entitled *Oryx*, and it was this society that initiated 'Operation Oryx' just before the launch of the World Wildlife Fund. This operation, which became the WWF's first major enterprise, consisted of an expedition aimed at capturing all remaining Arabian oryxes and bringing them into appropriate zoos, there to form a breeding nucleus. In time, the hope ran, large enough herds might be built up, from which the desert habitat could be restocked. The enterprise became the more urgent when it was learned, in 1962, that a hunting party had just killed forty-eight of the remaining oryxes, numbering between eighty and 100, and that they had then returned and killed sixteen more.

The planning and organization of the expedition were elaborate.

An oryx running in the Namib desert. Fleet of foot, the oryx's whereabouts can sometimes only be detected by the puffs of sand it raises

Nothing was left to chance. Under the leadership of Major J. R. Grimwood, assisted by a wide variety of specialists, everything possible was done to avoid traumatizing the animals in their capture and transportation. There were many snags and disappointments, not the least being a report, happily unfounded, that just before the party set off, the last of the oryxes had been killed; but the expedition proceeded in spite of this, in April to May 1962. Eventually three oryxes were brought back to Kenya and were then taken to the Maytag Zoo in Phoenix, Arizona. Although the group consisted of two males and a female, not the ideal proportions for starting a breeding herd, it was indeed a start.

The world herd

It may be sheer coincidence that these few oryxes, snatched from certain extinction, should have been taken to modern Phoenix, but the symbolism is of the happiest order. The phoenix was a mythical bird that appeared from the East every 500 years, built its nest, set fire to it, was itself reduced to ashes and three days later rose again, intact, from its ashes. To the three taken there was added a female donated by the London Zoo, four more animals were sent from Riyad Zoo by King Saud of Saudi Arabia, and another from the Ruler of Kuwait. The World Herd, as it was later named, now numbered four males and five females. In October 1963 the first lamb was born and another soon after, but sadly the first six were males.

The expedition was launched none too soon, for in 1972 D. S. Henderson, on a further expedition, found the remains of three oryxes and evidence of four more having been taken alive. These were almost certainly the last of the wild Arabian oryxes. Meanwhile, in the zoo at Phoenix all was going well, in fact so well that some of the oryxes were transferred to other zoos.

It is too often overlooked that, during all this time, there were small herds in captivity in various parts of Arabia—in Saudi Arabia and Abu Dhabi and, most importantly, a herd of a score or so in Qatar. The largest is, however, the World Herd at Phoenix and San Diego, which in July 1977 numbered eighty-two head in all.

An unromantic setting for these beautiful white antelopes, but all too necessary for the survival of the species

Whooping crane: *an experiment in fostering*

Fossil remains indicate that the whooping crane, four feet tall, white with black wingtips and red naked skin on the crown and cheeks, dates back some 500,000 years. It probably reached its zenith at the close of the last ice age, when the retreating glaciers left much of North America covered with grassy plains interspersed with marshes, numerous lakes and ponds. This was ideal habitat for cranes, and the whooping crane ranged over virtually the whole of the United States and southern Canada. But in time the water drained from the land and the forests spread, and by the time the first Europeans had settled in North America the numbers of cranes were down to an estimated 2000 or so.

As the continent was opened up and the land drained for the purpose of agriculture, the crane's habitat shrank still further. The large crane was a source of good palatable meat and numbers were shot for the table. The rarer the bird became the higher the price commanded for its skins and for the eggs sought after by collectors. Between 1870 and 1900 its numbers went down to less than 150, and by 1912 the surviving population consisted of between eighty and 100 birds. By 1940 the numbers were down to twenty-seven and six years later only twenty remained, one of these being in captivity.

Protection on the migration route

At this point conservationists became really alarmed. One of the adverse factors contributing to the crane's decline was that the bird is migratory, breeding in Canada and wintering in the southern United States, involving an annual two-way journey of 4400 miles with the continual risk of being shot at *en route*. Another adverse factor lay in the crane's strong territorial instinct, each pair of birds requiring 400 acres of territory for successful breeding. So space was needed, as well as protection from hunters and wildfowlers along the route, between the nesting and wintering grounds. The fight to save the whooping crane serves as a model of what can be done to save a vanishing species and the story of the measures taken is a romance containing many lessons to be applied now and in the future.

The first crusader on behalf of the whooping cranes was Robert Porter Allen of the American Audubon Society who spent his life studying the biology and migrations of the bird. In 1937 the United States Fish and Wildlife Service had taken over Blackjack Peninsula (since renamed the Aranas Wildlife Refuge) on the coast of Texas, as a wildfowl reserve. Within a few years it became apparent that this, and neighbouring marshes, was also the wintering ground of the few remaining whooping cranes, and that it could be used for their protection. The location of the summer breeding ground was, however, unknown and losses were still being incurred on the migration route. Thus, from 1949 to 1950, forty-three cranes wintered in Aranas and from 1952 to 1953 only twenty-one returned. The losses may have been due to natural causes—six had disappeared during a severe storm in the years of the Second World War— or to shooting. Taking no chances a massive propaganda campaign was mounted all along the migration route. Farmers were canvassed to avoid shooting this large white bird. Posters were displayed, showing a picture of the crane and how to identify it and notice boards were set up exhorting people not to shoot it. The success of the campaign is epitomized by the action of a farmer who, in 1958, shot one of these cranes, mistaking it for a snow goose. When he realized what he had done he surrendered himself to the police, was tried in court and fined 500 dollars.

Numbers counted on the wintering ground before and after the propaganda campaign	
BEFORE	
1870-1900	less than 150
1912 –	80-100
1940 –	27
1946 –	20
AFTER	
1952 –	28
1958 –	32
1961 –	38
1965 –	44
1969 –	50
1977 –	70

With the wintering ground protected and the migration route made reasonably safe, the next problem was to find the remaining breeding ground. The last nest had been seen in 1922 and no other was found until 1954, when after a prolonged aerial search nests were located, by a fortunate coincidence, in the Wood Buffalo Park in Canada, a reserve of 17,300 square miles of wilderness near the Great Slave Lake. This was Robert Allen's final triumph. After having flown 20,000 miles during 1948 and 1949 unsuccessfully, in search of breeding grounds, he learned that a helicopter returning from fire patrol in Canada's North West Territory had spotted a pair with one young.

Slow reproductive rate

The success of the propaganda campaign can also be judged by the numbers noted on the wintering grounds. In 1955 twenty-eight were counted, in 1958 thirty-two, in 1961 thirty-eight, in 1965 forty-four, in 1969 fifty. Bringing the census up to date, in 1977 seventy were counted, including seventeen breeding pairs. Even that number is still perilously low if one takes into account possible dangers such as disease, storms and other natural hazards, the danger from inbreeding and from the slow reproductive rate. The whooping crane does not start to breed until it is between four and five years old. Each female lays only two eggs, sometimes only one, and although there is a hatching success of eighty-five per cent, one out of every two chicks from a two-egg clutch dies within the first five months. At the Audubon Park Zoo in New Orleans a female, named Josephine, sole survivor from a flock caught in a hurricane, lived thirty years, laid fifty eggs of which only four chicks survived to maturity.

Although the wintering ground was apparently as safe as the nesting ground there were still fears for the safety of the birds. Oil-drilling taking place in the area was likely to disturb the birds and the offshore shell-dredging created silting, which might destroy the aquatic plants, crustacea and other invertebrates, as well as the frogs on which the cranes fed. Then came a further menace and although this was averted, the manner in which this was accomplished is highly illuminating. This came from the decision of the United States Air Force to use photoflash bombs, known to cause

Whooping cranes daintily picking their way across the ideal marshy habitat of the Aranas Wildlife Refuge in Texas

panic among wildlife, on a bombing range in an area adjacent to the Aranas Wildlife Refuge. The concerted efforts of conservationists to avert this were to no avail until finally they were taken to top diplomatic level: the Canadian ambassador took the matter direct to the American Secretary of State and the bombing range was sited elsewhere. That this matter was taken to ambassadorial level shows alone how deeply rooted is the desire on the part of the two North American neighbours to protect the crane.

Protection is, however, not enough. As long as the numbers of the crane remain at or near the present level there is always the possibility of the threats listed above wiping out the entire species in the foreseeable future. Two highly important schemes have, however, been put into action. One was to salvage the second chick from as many two-egg clutches as possible. The other was to try to establish a second, shorter, migratory route. The first concerns the normal losses among the chicks. In the mid-1950s Fred Bard, of the Regina Provincial Museum of Natural History, Saskatchewan, had put forward the idea of using sandhill cranes as foster parents for whooping crane chicks. This was taken up by Dr Rod Drewien, of the Wildlife Cooperative Research of the University of Idaho.

Sandhill crane as foster parent

The sandhill crane is about the same size as the whooping crane, but is grey and the two species are very similar in their biology. Like the whooper the sandhill breeds in the north and migrates south, but does so on a more westerly route, so although some sandhills winter in Texas the main wintering ground is in the western United States and Mexico. Drewien set to work in 1975 to collect one egg from every two-egg clutch of whoopers in the Wood Buffalo Park and fly them south to Grays Lake National Wildlife Refuge in Soda Springs, Idaho, where there is one of the largest sandhill nesting colonies. There the eggs, already partially incubated by the parent whooper, were placed one each under selected brooding sandhills. Only sandhills known, by means of banding, to winter in the Bosque del Apache National Wildlife Reserve were chosen.

Grown chicks migrate

In the first year, of the fourteen eggs transferred, nine hatched and six survived to the time for migration. These were banded and colour-marked for later recognition. The chicks, now well grown and able to fly, migrated with their foster parents to the sandhill cranes' wintering ground in Bosque del Apache. Two of the six surviving chicks were never seen again, presumably having perished on the journey. The other four were searched for and located among the 10,000 or more sandhills that winter there.

In 1976 these same young whoopers travelled north on the spring migration with the foster parents. They were seen resting together in the Monte Vista National Wildlife Park, half-way between Bosque del Apache and Grays Lake Wildlife reserves, the normal stopping place for the sandhills, but when the foster parents set off for Grays Lake the young whoopers remained behind because the time had come when sandhill parents normally reject their growing chicks. This was disappointing because it had been hoped that the young whoopers would have reached Grays Lake before their foster parents rejected them. There is, nevertheless, still the hope that a new migration route for whooping cranes will have been established, but because the young birds will take four to five years to mature the fostering experiment will have to be continued until 1980, or later, before it will be known whether success or failure has resulted.

In 1977, fifteen chicks hatched out of sixteen eggs from Wood Buffalo Park and five chicks were reared out of fourteen eggs brought from a captive flock at the Patuxent Research Station.

A sandhill foster parent. Used in an experiment to try and increase numbers of the fast-disappearing whooper, the sandhill, though of different colouring and slightly different size, is biologically similar. Success or failure of the project will not be known until 1980

Discoveries: *rediscoveries and rare achievements*

Conservation in any form tends to be a depressing business because it is an eternal struggle between altruists and those motivated by selfish interests. This is a situation in which overnight the efforts of a thousand well-wishers can be offset at the stroke of a pen by one individual who is either actuated by greed or is merely ignorant. Even so, there are always gleams or flashes of hope. As far as animals are concerned these are represented by such things as the discovery of an animal hitherto unknown or the rediscovery of one thought to have become extinct.

As to new discoveries the larger the animal brought to light for the first time the greater the excitement (certainly in the Press), although a professional zoologist can get just as excited over a new animal the size of a pinhead as over one the size of a gigantosaurus! Unhappily, the days are fairly certainly past when we could expect the news of a large unknown animal to catalogue. By contrast, new species are being recorded every year and have been since systematic registering of the animal kingdom began. The great majority are invertebrates, some are fishes, amphibians and reptiles. The chance of a bird unknown to science turning up is remote, but the same is not true of mammals.

Flightless teal

There has long been doubt as to whether the flightless teal, living on Campbell island, nearly 400 miles to the south of New Zealand, still existed. It was thought, in 1949, that there might be a dozen or two left, but there had been no positive record of one since 1944. There had been an unconfirmed sighting in 1958, but in 1976 it was seen again and this time for certain.

The flightless teal, recently seen after it had been thought to be on the verge of extinction

Peregrine falcon

The peregrine falcon, the most coveted bird in falconry, was the hardest hit by the pesticide DDT, which induced sterility, the eggs failing to hatch. In some parts of its range the whole population was wiped out. In 1976 Cornell University's Laboratory of Ornithology released forty-two peregrines, hatched in captivity, bringing the total released since 1974 to sixty-two. The expectation is that 100 or more may be produced in 1977 and 200 in 1978.

Honeycreeper

The family Drepanididae is reserved solely for the Hawaiian honeycreepers and at its zenith it contained ten genera, twenty-three species and twenty-four subspecies, with such attractive vernacular names as 'O'u, 'Apapane, 'Amakiki and Nuku-pu'u. Some forty per cent have become extinct in the last century or so, twenty-five per cent of the remainder are listed as endangered and one species is now thought to be extinct. Yet in 1973 a species new to science, the Po'o-uli (*Melamprosops phaeosoma*), was discovered.

The splendid peregrine falcon. All being well, chicks hatched in captivity will swell numbers of this species, sadly affected by DDT

Woolly monkey

The yellow-tailed woolly monkey of Peru, last seen in 1926, was feared extinct and was rediscovered in 1975 by Russell A. Mittelmeier, Hernando de Macedo Ruiz and Anthony Luscombe in the area of the lower Andes, where it had previously been seen. The three men brought back a living young one as well as three skulls and four skins, which they obtained from a local hunter, who shot the animals for food.

Cahow

The cahow is one of the gadfly petrels, medium-sized seabirds that nest on oceanic islands. Early settlers on Bermuda, where the cahow is native, found it in incredible numbers. They took its eggs and killed the bird for its palatable flesh. In the winter of 1614–15 there was starvation on the island and more and more cahows were killed. Finally, the governor issued an edict that no more were to be destroyed, but the order came too late. The cahow was virtually extinct.

In 1916 a bird was found, dead, and its skeleton was identical with the skeletons of cahows found in caves on the island. In 1931 a cahow flew into the St David's light and in 1944 another crashed into a telegraph pole. In 1951 Robert Cushman Murphy organized an expedition to look for cahow nests and six were found on cliffs. By 1967 twenty-two breeding pairs had been recorded, but they produced only eight young and the total population was estimated to be no more than eighty.

During 1971–5 a total of sixty-five young were reared. Then it was realized that the main threat to the cahow came from competition for nest sites from the white-tailed tropicbird. David Wingate, Bermuda's chief conservation officer, fixed baffles to all known cahow nesting burrows. These prevented the tropicbirds from using them, but allowed the smaller cahow to go in and out freely.

The white-tailed tropicbird nesting only a few inches away from a man-made baffle attached to the cahow's nesting burrow. This intriguing but simple device could mean a rescue from near-extinction for the rare cahow

Magpie robin

The magpie robin, a small black bird with white wing patches was once found on all the islands of the Seychelles group in the Indian Ocean. Then, in 1867, it was reported to be scarce on Mahe island, the largest and most populous of the group. After that it suffered a dramatic decline throughout the group of islands and in 1965 only twelve were found, on Frigate island. The bird is extremely tame and it feeds almost exclusively on the ground, so it fell an easy prey to introduced cats and rats. However, an expedition visiting Frigate island in 1973 counted thirty-eight, which represents nearly the maximum number, although it is possible that in spite of repeated counts two or three pairs might have been missed. It is quite likely that the magpie robin will make a comeback because the island's inhabitants (workers on the coconut plantations and the fruit and vegetable farms, and their families) are forming the habit of feeding the birds when they visit the houses.

Solenodon

Until a few years ago it was generally supposed that the two species of solenodon, the shrew-like insectivore, nearly two feet long, were doomed to extinction. Confined to Cuba and Haiti, solenodons were rarely seen and it was feared that the few remaining would be wiped out by their main enemies, domestic cats and dogs gone feral. Both solenodons are protected by law, but this is inoperative against domestic pets, especially those that have taken to living in the wild. In 1974–5, however, three were captured in two areas in Oriente Province, at the eastern end of Cuba. This led to a survey being made, which revealed that while the solenodon is thin on the ground it is more widespread than was supposed. This seems to have been common knowledge among local farmers, who were prepared not to molest the animals since they did no effective harm, their flesh, like true shrews, is unpalatable and their fur useless. Once attention was focused on this unusual and supposedly rare animal, as a result of the survey, there came an unexpected danger. According to Dr Luis S. Varona, consultant to the Fauna Preservation Society in Cuba, the local people who know where solenodons are to be found 'have been trying to capture them in order to see their names and photographs on television and in newspapers and magazines'. So ironically the solenodon was safer when everyone thought it was on the way to extinction. However, it is a protected animal and anyone capturing one and displaying it is liable to be ordered to take it back to the place where it was found and release it. This is sound sense not only for the treatment of solenodons but for other rare animals. Indeed, for the solenodon we might almost say 'protect me from my friends'.

Once common in the Seychelles group of islands, the magpie robin's numbers diminished rapidly at the mercy of cats and rats

Best left alone? This strange-looking animal has been an unfortunate victim of publicity which was intended to help save it

Top: one of the few remaining pairs of Mauritius kestrels. This species came uncomfortably close to extinction

Above: the mystery marsupial mouse is only four inches long from the tip of its nose to the end of its tail, which accounts almost for half its length

Mauritius kestrel

Several species of birds are reduced to a few pairs, but the Mauritius kestrel must have come as near extinction as any, without actually disappearing altogether. A century ago it was present in abundance; forty years ago it was common; in 1967 it was considered almost extinct. In 1977 two of the four remaining pairs successfully hatched four eggs between them. If the chicks from these live to breed themselves and adequate protection is given to the twelve, we may yet be able to notch up one more species that has been drawn back from the brink of extinction.

Marsupial mouse

In early 1975 a shrew-like marsupial mouse four inches long entered a trap in the Billaitt Conservation Park, a nature reserve 100 miles east of Adelaide, South Australia. It was a female with six young. The animal was studied before being named and described, a process that can take a very long time and currently it is not possible to give it a name. It is mentioned here because it set zoological pulses beating faster, largely because it is a marsupial, and although marsupials are found elsewhere in the world (especially in South America) the name has become linked with the collection of quaint and fascinating mammals that make up the bulk of the fauna of Australia. So there is a sort of aura associated with the mere word 'marsupial'.

As far as size is concerned the newcomer is no bigger than a mouse, and new species of mice not infrequently turn up in the traps set in the wild by zoological expeditions. A few years ago, for example, a new species of mouse was discovered in Africa in an area of marshland and could be found nowhere else. Although it excited no headlines it is zoologically important and certainly interesting.

Even as this is being written comes the news that a rat-sized rodent, new to science, has been photographed on a mountain north of Cairns in northern Queensland, Australia, and there are doubtless many more mouse- or rat-sized rodents yet to come to light.

There is, if anything, even more joy in the conservation world when a species believed extinct is found to be still extant, or even when a species on the verge of extinction is found to be increasing in numbers once again. This is almost as stimulating as the discovery of a new species, and these few examples have been given to illustrate how the discovery has been made and what were the factors contributing to it.

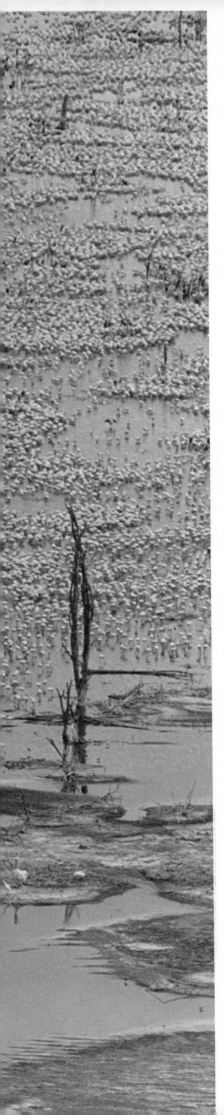

ON THE BRINK OF EXTINCTION

Flamingo Aye-aye Deer Gharial
Kouprey Zebra Cheetah Giant sable

This section has a somewhat discouraging tale to tell. It outlines some of the sad losses in terms of near-extinction which have occurred when it has been realized, much too late, that an animal is on the verge of vanishing forever.

Steps have subsequently been taken to save the animal in jeopardy, but plans have frequently misfired due to mismanagement of one kind or another.

Sometimes the animal has become a victim of political wrangling; money has been donated, only to be withdrawn or the habitat of the animal has been all but destroyed before anything can be done to change the habits and practices of the local people, who may rely on the surroundings for their own livelihood.

The flamingos on Lake Nakuru, in Kenya's Great Rift Valley, have quite rightly been acclaimed as one of the greatest ornithological spectacles on earth, but unfortunately they are in the process of being scattered over other lakes in the area because of pollution. The rare and shy aye-aye has been a victim of deforestation. Several species of deer have been hunted virtually to extinction or have otherwise suffered through man's destruction of the habitat. The gharial, the most primitive crocodilian, has fallen foul of both primitive practices and the modernization of the environment.

Most commonly, of course, animals have been hunted quite ruthlessly for their skins. The unfortunate zebra and cheetah have both been hunted or poached in order to supply a ready demand for their hides.

A mass of flamingos on the shores of Lake Nakuru, Kenya

Flamingo: *Nakuru's disappearing spectacle*

Lake Nakuru, with its myriad pink flamingos, in Kenya's Great Rift Valley, has been rightly acclaimed the greatest ornithological spectacle on earth. In the light of present events, however, that spectacle may be on the verge of extinction. The flamingos themselves may not be lost, but the Nakuru spectacle itself may be, since the birds are mobile and can disperse themselves over the smaller lakes strung along the valley. As conditions on the lake have varied, their numbers have continually fluctuated between 50,000 and over one million. To understand this one needs to examine the physical features of the lake itself, the history of conservation measures taken and the socio-political changes likely to end this spectacle.

Fluctuating water level

The lake is 10,000 acres in extent. It is 6000 feet above sea level, has no outlet and is fed by five rivers. Like other lakes in the Rift Valley, it represents a low sump point in the surrounding country. Its average depth is between three and four feet, its greatest depth between eight and nine feet, and its water level tends to fluctuate with the average annual rainfall. Its maximum depth in 1972 was eight feet, in 1973 it was six feet, in 1974 it was five feet, in three successive years of below-average rainfall. In succeeding years the situation has been aggravated by changes in land usage, causing erosion and the silting of the rivers.

On the northern border stands the town of Nakuru, which in 1963 numbered 25,000 inhabitants. Its population has increased to over 70,000 in fourteen years. The population of Kenya itself, less than two million at the beginning of this century, now stands at thirteen million and is estimated to reach double that figure in the next nineteen years. This pressure of population means more settlement of the land generally, the

A crowd of lesser flamingos in the shallows. Lake Nakuru attracted this species of flamingo in particular because of the alga Spirulina platensis, *which formed its principal diet*

destruction of forests for fuel and to supply agricultural land, more erosion and therefore no lessening of the silting process.

Kenya's good intentions

Kenya, out of all the African states, certainly among those newly independent, is regarded justifiably as the most advanced in matters of conservation. For example, all hunting was banned in mid-1977—although this does not mean the end of the major evil, poaching—but it is evidence of good intent. It is also evidence that the government is acutely aware that only ten per cent of game animals remain in East Africa.

Birdlife protection

These figures, combined with the magnificent flamingo spectacle, have influenced the conservation measures taken. The southern section of the lake came under National Parks' protection in 1961. The whole lake and its foreshores became a National Park in 1968 and three years later the area of the park was trebled to protect as much as possible the surrounding ecosystem, which included savannah and bush and three large areas of forest. Lake Nakuru is the first National Park in Africa to be established primarily to protect birdlife, which aside from the flamingos, is both prolific and spectacular and includes 400 species. The rest of the fauna is not negligible, including as it does fifty species of mammals, of which the hoofed animals are 1400 Defassa waterbuck, 1200 impala, 500 Thomson's gazelle, 250 Cape buffalo and 150 Bohar reedbuck. Other inhabitants of the extended Nakuru National Park worthy of note are at least six pairs of leopards, a group of rhinoceros and a small herd of twenty-four zebra, which entered the park and took up residence.

Such was the importance attached to the new park that it was selected as the focal point for the country-wide activities to mark the United Nations' World Environment Day, on June 5 1974. It was then that the expanded park was officially opened with an inauguration ceremony attended by His

Flamingo

Excellency the Vice President of Kenya, four of Kenya's cabinet ministers, the Minister of State in the President's Office, the Attorney-General, the Minister for Tourism, the Minister for National Resources and other dignitaries of national and local government, together with over 20,000 of Nakuru's citizens. Shops, offices and factories were closed for the day. Clearly, this was a great occasion, and deservedly so, for already every effort had been exerted to avoid that arch-menace, pollution. A new site had been found for Nakuru's municipal dump, in a fissure caused by the rifting effect of the Great Rift Valley. Factory waste had been dealt with. The sewage farm that had served the town adequately when the population figures had been low was being replaced by a larger farm. This had been made possible by a promised loan of 4m DM from the Federal Republic of West Germany, at a low rate of interest.

World Wildlife Fund donation

An educational unit had been set up in the Baharini Wildlife Sanctuary at the northern end of the lake adjacent to the town, in conjunction with the already-existing research station. The World Wildlife Fund had donated £172,500 for the purchase of the land to extend the park. The local youth movements had combined to clean up the site of the old municipal dump, which is now covered with a fine growth of trees.

Threat to alga

Then the blow fell. It was proposed to establish a factory on the edge of the town for the manufacture of pesticides, especially of copper oxychloride for the control of coffee berry disease, a fungus-based disease. Copper in the proportions of five parts per million is lethal to algal growth, and the flamingos depended on the unusually rich growth, especially of a blue-green alga *Spirulina platensis*, which made up ninety-five per cent of all algae in the lake and formed the principal diet of Nakuru's famous lesser flamingos, *Phoeniconaias minor*. It is also the basis of all the lake's food chains. The importance of this alga was made evident by what happened in 1974, when a marked change in the lake's algal flora took place when the water level fell as the result of three successive years of low rainfall. *Spirulina* disappeared and its place was taken by a small green alga *Chlamydomonas*. This alga is too small for the lesser flamingo to filter out and about ninety per cent of the birds left Lake Nakuru and dispersed themselves on other East African lakes and possibly as far away as South Africa. The great ornithological spectacle was temporarily at an end.

Pesticide factory built

The decision to establish the pesticide factory was taken without consultation with the appropriate authorities. Even the Water Department was kept in ignorance. Once the decision was made public protests came from all those knowledgeable in conservation and a high-level government enquiry was instituted; but all was in vain. It can only be supposed that money speaks, even in high places—unless it happens to be the hard-won cash of the World Wildlife Fund! The building of the factory went ahead despite a legalized agreement between government and WWF that the money donated by WWF was to be used to 'safeguard the ecology of the lake from man-made pollution'.

The new sewage farm, which was to replace the already over-strained original one, ran into difficulties. The loan from the government of West Germany was to be made available in instalments as first one section was completed, then another. Finally, as the result of delays and procrastination over half the 4m DM offered were withdrawn.

Right: greater flamingos bickering over nesting space

Aye-aye: *a mysterious and vanishing lemur*

The large island of Madagascar, now Malagasy, lies off the southeastern tip of Africa. It is the home of the aye-aye and if any animal can be said to be steeped in mystery it is this one. Malagasy became separated from Africa as the southern part of the world's land mass drifted apart to give rise to the large and small fragments of Africa, Australia and the East Indies. The special feature of Malagasy was that it contained, in the forests that formerly covered it, the ancestral stock from which, in the course of time, sprang the order of the Primates: lemurs, monkeys, apes and man.

Man eventually spread himself over the whole earth, while the apes only managed to reach the tropical parts of what are now Africa and Asia. The monkeys did better, but still only ranged over the tropical regions of the world. The lemurs also lived in Africa, where their fossils have been found, but their descendants survived only on Malagasy, largely because monkeys and apes never reached the island to compete for food and living space.

Then came man, 1500 years ago, to settle on the island, where lived the fabled roc or elephant bird, the pygmy hippo, a giant tortoise and the families of lemurs, including some the size of gorillas. Some of the many species that made up what was virtually a museum of animal oddities died out naturally, but the demise of many can be laid at the door of the early settlers and their descendants. The roc finally became extinct in the mid-seventeenth century. It was followed by, among other quaint or unique animal species, fourteen of the thirty-three species of lemurs.

Elusive nocturnal animal

The one species among the surviving lemurs that has attracted most scientific attention is the aye-aye, because of its specialized character. It has also been the most elusive. About the size of a domestic cat, with long legs and a mainly black coat, a bushy fox-like tail, large ears and eyes, it is completely nocturnal; it does not emerge from its nest high in the trees until after dark, but it may then come down to the ground. It is also shy and secretive, quick to react to human presence and take evasive action, and impossible to keep for long in a zoo because of the difficulty of providing its specialized food. Efforts to photograph it in the wild have only been partially successful, the best results, until recently, being due to the painstaking and prolonged attempts of Professor J. J. Petter, who has been responsible for establishing, in 1966, a sanctuary for the aye-aye on the tiny island of Nosy Mangabe, in the northeastern corner of Malagasy.

In 1975 Elizabeth Bomford, winner of the Great Wildlife Photographic Adventure, used her prize to visit Malagasy and Nosy Mangabe in quest of the aye-aye. We are grateful for the vivid story she has told of her night excursions in the dense forest, hoping to see and photograph the animal and of her graphic account of the spoliation of Malagasy and its causes.

Burning the forest

Malagasy, the fifth-largest island in the world, 228,000 square miles, with a population today of seven million people, mainly African in origin, was originally covered with virgin forest. It was taken over as a protectorate by the French in 1895 and it achieved independence in 1960. Today its chief crops are coffee, vanilla, cloves and pepper and its cattle are zebu. To provide the land for agriculture and husbandry the age-old method of burning forest was followed. When the soil was exhausted more forest was burnt and today, in order to provide fresh fodder for livestock, areas of mature grassland are burned so that the cattle can feed on the fresh young grass growing up through the ashes.

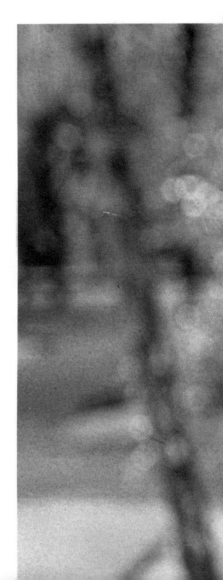

The French botanists realized that this island, with its unique flora, which included many fine orchids, was in danger from this method of exploiting the soil and in the 1920s the first Reserves Naturelles Integrales were established. Little attention was paid to the equally interesting fauna and although roads and railways were built and a system of education established, the local children were taught only French history and geography. Such education as they had in natural history concerned only the plants and animals of other countries and it seems that field guides to the native flora and fauna do not exist. It is not surprising, therefore, that the local inhabitants have only their limited folklore, largely based on superstition, to guide them and no appreciation of the value of their unique wildlife, which could help to encourage tourism, let alone of the need to conserve anything except for immediate use. The attitude also prevails that what lives and grows locally is their property.

The need for education

It is self-evident that conservation can only succeed when the need for it in general, and in particular, is appreciated at the grassroots by the ordinary people. Governments can decree what they like, but to no effect if the local people do not co-operate. Half the present population consists of children under fourteen, so there is not only the need for education, but a great opportunity for it. But Malagasy, newly independent, has many problems of more immediate urgency, and with so high a percentage of juveniles in the country survival is one of them. Meanwhile the lemurs in general and the aye-aye in particular are having their habitat destroyed.

The shy and secretive aye-aye, about the same size as a domestic cat, is a nocturnal animal and quick to take evasive action in the presence of man

Elizabeth Bomford saw only two aye-ayes in spite of her courageous efforts—it certainly takes courage to camp alone on a jungle-covered island and venture out at night surrounded by darkness and the strange calls of nocturnal animals, including the loud cat-like yowling of the ruffed lemur. This jungle-covered island was Nosy Mangabe, wisely chosen by Jean Jacques Petter to be the haven for the aye-aye. It is reached by a sea crossing over water rough enough to discourage most local fishermen in their dugout canoes. The island is also taboo because of the ancestral tombs on it—knowledge of which must add considerably to the nervous stress of someone exploring the forest alone at night, no matter how level-headed they are! On the mainland, also, sites of tombs are surrounded by areas of untouched forest, forming small pockets of conservation.

Crouched under a pile of leaves, the aye-aye peers about in the staring, wide-eyed manner characteristic of many nocturnal animals

Unknown fate

Mrs Bomford reported seeing only two aye-ayes altogether, and one of these was in captivity on the mainland. Nine had been transported to Nosy Mangabe in 1966, in the hope that they would survive and breed, saving the species from extinction. Nobody knows their fate. They may have bred. There are several instances of animals being considered rare until someone, perhaps for an entirely different purpose, takes the trouble to look around. Like the G.I. stationed in Panama during the Second World War who found the local sloths, thought to be rare, so numerous that there was almost one in every tree. So although Mrs Bomford suspects that at most there could be only two or three aye-ayes on Nosy Mangabe, the situation may be better than she fears. One cannot but agree when she remarked that after ten years it did not appear to be a vigorous breeding population, even taking into account the aye-aye's slow reproductive rate.

Should the aye-aye become extinct through the deforestation of Malagasy, no country can point the accusing finger. For example, there are approximately three million square miles of tropical rain forest in South America, Africa and Southeast Asia, and fourteen acres of tropical forest are being cut down every minute. A similar process has been going on in the northern hemisphere for centuries—and we still waste paper!

Deer: *nine endangered species*

The most coveted animal is almost certainly the deer. In medieval Europe it was the favourite animal for the chase and kings and nobles jealously guarded their deer parks. The common man risked hanging for poaching deer, yet he continued to do so to feed his family, if for no other reason. Deer-poaching continues into this modern age even in advanced countries and affluent societies. Elsewhere in the world other uses are found for deer, in addition to taking their flesh for meat and using their hides. Not surprisingly, therefore, a third of all the kinds of deer are endangered, several having a total population of 100 or less. Listed below is a selection of those living nearest the extinction line, sufficient to show the factors that have brought some species of deer to a low ebb in different parts of the world.

The Persian fallow deer always had a limited range. It is found only in Iran, where its total population is now probably less than fifty.

The Manipur deer, counted from the air in a sanctuary in India, numbered fourteen in 1975; five stags, six hinds and three fawns. Even these were threatened by grazing of domestic stock and poaching, as well as by the building of the Log Tak dam, which threatens to change the habitat of the deer quite dramatically by raising the water level.

Pampas deer, once found in great numbers in South America, were hunted for their skins, thousands being exported in the late nineteenth century

Left: the hangul or Kashmir deer, of India, now preserved in captivity, fell victim to the spoliation of its habitat

The hangul or Kashmir deer, of India, numbered about 150 in 1974, in the Dachigam sanctuary in the mountains. Sheep are reared in the sanctuary, buffaloes and goats graze there leading to the destruction of the habitat—goats especially have been responsible in many parts of the world for reducing a floral paradise to desert. Military personnel stationed in the area have also taken toll of the hangul.

Threat from tree-felling

Another subspecies of the red deer, closely related to Kashmir deer and also called the hangul is the Bokharan deer. It lives in forests in the USSR, confined to an area on the Turkmenistan-Afghanistan frontier, which is constantly under threat from tree-felling. In 1971 it was estimated to number fewer than 500, but in 1977 a more careful count put the figure at double this.

In 1938 the barasingha, or southern swamp deer, numbered over 3000 in the Kanha National Park in central India. In 1970 the numbers were down to seventy, but rose to ninety-six in 1972 and to over 100 in 1973. By 1974 the figure had risen to between 130 and 140, largely the result of the removal of a village inside the park and the resettlement of the villagers outside.

Unchecked hunting

The shou, a subspecies of the Eurasian red deer or wapiti, formerly ranged through Bhutan and southeastern Tibet in fair numbers. In 1971 it was reported to be reduced to 100 by uncontrolled hunting by local villagers, sportsmen and Chinese military personnel. In 1976 the Bhutanese Forest Department made extensive searches and came to the conclusion that the shou was extinct in Bhutan. A few may have survived in adjacent areas in Tibet.

McNeill's deer, yet another subspecies of the red deer, living on the Tibetan plateau and neighbouring Szechwan, was for years thought to be extinct. There is, however, a small population remaining. Like several other Asiatic deer it has been overhunted for its veleted antlers, the

The graceful barasingha, or southern swamp deer, seen here wading in the swamp that is its natural habitat

substance of which has been used by the Chinese as an aphrodisiac.

Still in Asia, Schomburgk's deer, of Thailand, had unusual antlers, which became coveted trophies. The deer is believed to have become extinct at some time between 1932 and 1939. Since then several expeditions have sought it in vain.

Victimized venado

The venado, the most southerly of the three species of pampas deer, used to be extremely abundant on the pampas of central Argentina until 1900. In 1977 the total population numbered about eighty. One of the biggest factors in this decline was hunting the deer for its skin. Other factors are the destruction of the habitat, poaching, competition with domestic livestock for the available fodder and diseases, including foot-and-mouth, contracted from farm and ranch animals. Some idea of the former numbers of the venado can be gauged from trade figures of exports, which show an average of 200,000 skins a year in the latter part of the nineteenth century.

The magnificent shou. Once reasonably common in Bhutan and southeastern Tibet it has now been made virtually extinct by unrestricted hunting

Gharial: *India's 'Loch Ness monster'*

The long-nosed crocodilian known as the gharial, or gavial, lives in the rivers of northern India. It is the most primitive crocodilian alive today, the last of many species that once inhabited the area. It is therefore a living fossil, a relic from the past, in a sense the Loch Ness monster of India, except that it really does exist. The comparison is justified, for if or when the 'monster' were ever shown to be real flesh and blood the most strenuous and urgent measures would be taken to ensure its survival. By contrast, the gharial has been declared to be in danger of imminent extinction, a fact that passes unnoticed by the world at large. For our present purpose the gharial functions as a singularly good example of how primitive practices and the modernization of the environment combine to stack the cards heavily against an animal species.

This unfortunate gharial, unprotected as its descendants are today, was found to have silver bangles, rings and a complete baby in its stomach

The gharial, being essentially a fish-eater, lacks some of the more

unpleasant features of the true crocodile, especially in the danger to human life and limb. There are, for example, no statistics about human victims and if it is in any sense a danger to the local peoples of the river system of the Ganges and its tributaries authors are noticeably reticent about it. Naturally, in such a large river system there are fishermen living along the banks, and a fish-eating reptile must inevitably be regarded as competitor for a limited food supply. So long as the fishermen use traditional methods of fishing the pressure on the gharial is not intense. Technological advancement, however, has brought the nylon net into the area which is set, complete with floats and sinkers, in the evening. The gharial becomes entangled in the net, which is expensive, and the reptile may damage it in its efforts to escape. Consequently, the fishermen have no compunction in clubbing any such captives to death.

Disturbed habitat

One of the tributaries, the Gandak river, passes through a densely populated agricultural area, but its eastern bank forms the boundary of the Royal Chitwan National Park, which should indicate 'sanctuary', especially since, for most of the year, the park is closed for grazing. However, a riverine grass grows in the area and the local inhabitants are not restricted from harvesting it, for thatching, between mid-January and mid-February. They transport it by boat and during this period the gharial's habitat is much disturbed. This would not necessarily matter except that the reptile has the incurable habit of basking on the river banks.

Basking a hazard

We do not know how far the basking habit contributes to the welfare of the beast, but since it is a conspicuous part of the daily life of crocodilians, it may reasonably be assumed that it is essential to them, and when one considers how widespread the habit is, among cold- and warm-blooded animals alike, it seems obvious that it is important to health. The gharial certainly makes a strong habit of it and, moreover, has a tendency to return repeatedly to the same spot to indulge it. This leads to another hazard. The Tharus, a local tribe living along the banks of the Gandak river, drive iron hooks into the gharial's pathway from the basking site. When hooked in

An effort to protect gharials in the Narayani river area, Chitwan, Nepal. Before the eggs can be gathered by the local people for food, they are collected and put into sand-filled boxes for safe transportation

this grisly fashion the reptile is speared and its flesh eaten.

Gharials, more strongly aquatic than most crocodilians, must also leave the water to breed and this leads to another danger. The females lay their eggs in the three-foot-deep pits they dig, younger gharials laying from twenty to thirty and the older ones up to sixty. They do this at night, but the tracks left by a female lead the egg-hunter without hesitation to the site of a nest. The eggs are eaten fried.

Unsuitable embankments

The Kosi river, coming down from the Nepalese Himalayas, used to be teeming with gharials which spread out with the flood waters over the countryside. According to S. P. Shahi, formerly Chief Conservator of Forests, who has made a strong appeal for protection of the gharial, these days are past. The river is now confined to prevent flooding and the gharials have been driven into a ghetto, causing their numbers to fall drastically. In addition the natural sandbanks, characteristic of these rivers, are largely being replaced by sloping concrete embankments, which make them unsuitable for basking and for egg-laying.

However, the main cause of the animal's decline, according to a report received by the World Wildlife Fund in 1974, from Romulus Whitaker, Director of the Madras Snake Park, is killing for its skin. 'Gharials are shot at, netted and prevented from basking in all but the most remote places, and today there are very few spots free from commercial fishing and other river activities.' Presumably there is implied here an indictment of the skin-hunters, although, ironically, the export of crocodile skin from India has been banned since 1958.

The practical effect of these adverse factors is highlighted by a survey

Below: taking the precious egg-filled boxes up the Narayani river to the hatchery

Below right: the eggs are transferred to a special hatchery at Chitwan

made by H. R. Bustard, during May to July 1974. He reported that all three Indian crocodilians are endangered. In his opinion the marsh crocodile, or mugger, is in danger of becoming extinct by 1995, the saltwater crocodile in less than twenty years and the gharial is already on the way out. In the Chambal river, for example, eighteen young gharials were killed in 1972 and seven large individuals in 1974, leaving at most between ten and fifteen, all told, in the river.

Diminishing fast

Shahi also quotes from a survey carried out from 1973 to 1974 by the Madras Snake Park Trust, covering Nepal as well as India, when only six gharials were seen, 'the fact that we were unable to see more than a few gharials, after extensive stays at river stretches described as teeming with crocodilians forty years ago, indicates the rapid change that has taken place'.

The same author cites the findings for the Mahanadi river, in Orissa, the only other known area, outside the Ganges basin, for the gharial. A stretch of this river passing through the Satkosia gorge has long been a stronghold for the species. Bustard's survey revealed a population reduced to five; three females and two males. Since the local people, the Matia, collect the eggs for food, the chances of any gharials remaining there by the late 1980s is remote indeed.

Following this survey Shahi decided to survey that part of the Gandak river in the area of Bihar and adjacent areas in Nepal. Here the Rapti river joins the Gandak. Where the two meet fourteen gharials had been observed in May 1973, but in January 1975 he saw only one.

Competing with the tiger

Given a protected area, which is not the same as being protected by law, this unique crocodilian could readily be preserved, judging by an experience of the local officials, who in April 1975 confiscated 134 eggs from a Tharu egg-collector. These were incubated in a sand mound and sixty hatched in June and July, the rest being infertile. Despite all efforts it is possible that the gharial has been left out in the cold by the attention given to the campaign to protect the tiger in much the same area, for it has complete protection under India's Wildlife Protection Act of 1972.

The most primitive crocodilian in existence, the gharial is a relic from the past. It has a remarkable gape and a formidable set of teeth, but it is essentially a fish-eater and is not a known danger to man

Kouprey: *grim outlook for a giant forest ox*

The last large land animal to be discovered (that is, made known to science) was the kouprey, the giant forest ox of Cambodia. This was in 1957. Twelve years later Dr Pierre Pfeffer, who had been keeping watch on the status of the animal, reported that there were only about twenty-three in the reserve on the Vietnam frontier, forty in the reserve bordering the frontiers with Laos and Thailand and possibly a few in a third reserve. He gave it as his opinion that the kouprey was then 'in as serious a danger as any animal in the world' and that the reserves no longer gave sanctuary. There was the suggestion to capture some of them and start a captive breeding unit in a safe place in Cambodia and another overseas.

The Cambodian government approved the plan. The Food and Agriculture Organization representative of the United Nations was ready to help, as was the International Union for the Conservation of Nature. War intervened as well as political changes in Cambodia. The one, very small, favourable aspect of the war was that by 1974 it had 'put a stop to the motorized poaching organized by government officials'!

Destruction of the forest

The following year an expedition reached the mountains of southeast Thailand, on the Cambodian frontier, to look for the kouprey. They saw none, although hunters reported having seen it. What the expedition found was destruction of the forest and with it the habitat of the kouprey. A road had been driven into the mountains to bring out lumber, trees were being felled continuously, plantations of maize and tapioca were multiplying, the forests were changing from evergreen to deciduous as the land was being increasingly settled. Shooting was heard at night, the parties of hunters using powerful flashlights.

The Thai government was prepared to make the Dongrak forest a national reserve, but the whole area had been allocated in timber leases and since then the political situation of the area has changed. The outlook for the last large land animal to be discovered must be grim indeed.

Zebra: *sad plight of a handsome animal*

Except for the dog and the cat, the horse has been the closest animal to civilized man, but whereas the first two are today best known as pets, the horse has always been utilized. As with all domesticated animals, its ancestors were originally wild, but whereas there is still some doubt as to which wild species gave us the domestic dog and the household cat, there is little doubt about the family tree of the horse.

The forest tarpan lived in the wooded areas of western, central and eastern Europe until the Middle Ages, when it became extinct. The steppe tarpan hung on in southeastern Europe until the nineteenth century. Przewalski's horse, sometimes called the Mongolian wild horse, the third subspecies of wild horse, inhabited the steppes and semi-deserts of southern Siberia, Mongolia and western China. It is also probably now extinct in the wild although occasional sightings are reported for the Gobi desert. There are, however, a hundred or more in captivity, with breeding herds in the zoological gardens in Prague, the United States (Catskill), the United Kingdom (Whipsnade) and Munich. There are also small herds in a semi-wild state in the Soviet Union. How far any of these are of pure stock is open to question, since the wild horse and feral domestic horses readily interbreed.

Summarized, the history of the modern horse is of a rapid decrease of its numbers in the wild as the numbers of its domesticated relatives have increased. The same has been true of a second member of the horse family,

Above: *zebra in southern Africa*

Below left: *Chapman's zebra at a waterhole by Etosha Pan, southwest Africa*

Below right: *a striking group of Burchell's zebra*

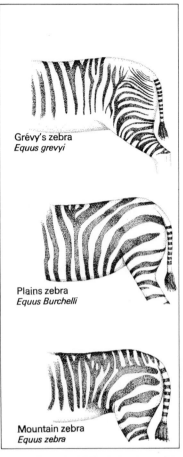

Grévy's zebra
Equus grevyi

Plains zebra
Equus Burchelli

Mountain zebra
Equus zebra

the wild ass, which gave us the donkey. There are two species of wild ass, the African and the Asian, each with several subspecies. While the donkey (the domestic ass) has been taken virtually all over the world and exists in large numbers, the various strains of wild asses have at best only a toehold on survival. Nevertheless, the toehold of the Asiatic wild ass has strengthened. Formerly widespread from the Syrian to the Gobi deserts, it is found now mainly in two reserves in the Soviet Union, and a census taken in 1974 showed that its numbers had increased from a few dozen to the substantial figure of 800.

It has been necessary to recapitulate a well-known story of two members of the horse family to emphasize that while as wild species they went downhill they were preserved in some form of domestication as well as in captivity. Moreover, their steep decline in the wild was the result of reasonable and logical utilization. No such argument can be advanced for the decline of the third member of the horse family, the zebra.

This is purely an African animal and, although formerly there was confusion about how many species survived into modern times, it is now accepted that four species should be recognized: Grévy's zebra of northeastern Africa; Burchell's, or the common zebra, of eastern to southern Africa; the mountain zebra of South Africa; the quagga and bontequagga, subspecies of a South African species that became extinct in the late nineteenth or early twentieth century. As we go from one species to the next the story becomes more and more depressing. The loss of the quagga and bontequagga represents, to begin with, a truly lamentable state of affairs. The quagga, especially, existed in herds of tens of thousands all

over the South African veldt. It was slaughtered for its hide and meat, to feed the Hottentot servants, and later the survivors of the herds were killed just for the sake of it. Today, of course, there is universal regret that this should have happened. One expression of this has been the evident pleasure with which isolated reports of alleged sightings were received during the second quarter of the twentieth century. These, unfortunately, were based on people seeing zeedonks, hybrids between a zebra and a domestic donkey. The quagga was half zebra, half ass, like a donkey in the rear half and a zebra up front.

The mountain zebra was never so numerous, but it is more by accident than design that it did not disappear completely. There are two subspecies, the Cape mountain zebra and Hartmann's zebra. The first of these has never occurred outside Cape Province, South Africa, and even there it never existed in large numbers. It was nothing more malicious than the spread of human settlement that virtually exterminated the subspecies before conservation measures were taken. Then, in 1937, it was estimated that no more than forty-five remained. In that year the Mountain Zebra

Mountain zebras have the distinctive feature of a fold of skin hanging from the throat. Unlike other species it runs together with its own kind and will not cross territory with another species

National Park was established, at Cradock, for five stallions and one mare. By 1950 all these had died, but eleven more were introduced from farms, where the few survivors had been enclosed by the landowners. Today there are fewer than 200 Cape mountain zebra all told: 130 at Cradock, a dozen in the De Hoop Provincial Nature Reserve and small herds in the Gamka, Attaqua, Outeniqua, Kamanassie and Kouga mountain ranges. The only real threat now to the Cape mountain zebra is that, should a disease break out, there are too few of them to provide viable survivors.

Hartmann's mountain zebra was more widespread. It formerly ranged through the coastal regions of Angola, south of latitude 14°S and through Namibia (southwest Africa) to Little Namaqualand, in South Africa itself. Again we have the same distressing story from the latter part of the nineteenth century, and by 1900 it was virtually extinct in South Africa. There were, however, still between 50,000 and 75,000 in Namibia, although in Angola numbers were dropping and by 1973 the only place to find them was in the Iona Game Reserve. The total numbers were down to 15,000 by 1960, down to 7000 by 1970 and by 1977 this figure had been

A baby zeedonk with its donkey mother. Hybrids between a zebra and a domestic donkey, zeedonks were mistaken for the now extinct quagga, a cross between a zebra and an ass

maintained. The decline of Hartmann's zebra is attributable to the animal's competition with man and his livestock. Today political unrest and the resulting supply of firearms to irresponsible people once again threatens the very existence of the subspecies.

Caught on the run: Grévy's zebra. Both Grévy's and Burchell's zebra share a common ancestor and today they run together

Grévy's range

At the other end of the continent, Grévy's zebra formerly ranged from southern Ethiopia and Somalia to northern Kenya, but today the only sizeable populations are in Kenya, where in 1971 it was estimated there were 10,000. Now numbers are estimated at under 1000. The species is extinct in Somalia and although a few individuals were seen in Ethiopia in 1972 it is unlikely there are any remaining there today. In Kenya, until 1976, licences to kill Grévy's could be bought for 246 dollars and in that year one hunter is reported to have taken out licences to kill 200. Fortunately, in 1977, the Kenyan government announced a ban on hunting zebras. In addition, Don Hunt of the Mount Kenya Game Ranch currently plans, with government backing, to catch 140 Grévy's zebras and take forty to the Samburu reserve and 100 to the Tsavo West park. It is also suggested that some others should be sent to zoos and ranches in South Africa and the United States. In 1976, the last year for which figures are presently available, there were 176 Grévy's in zoos outside Kenya: twenty-six mares and three stallions at Dvur in Czechoslovakia, fourteen mares and nine stallions at Tampa in the United States and about thirty beasts in two zoos in the United Kingdom. Conservationists predict that the species will be extinct in the wild by 1980.

Flourishing trade

The common Burchell's zebra is still found over a wide area in eastern and southern Africa (see map) and is not yet an endangered species. This comfortable situation could, however, be radically altered if political changes in subsaharan Africa are not achieved peacefully and, more especially, if hunting and poaching pressures are not drastically reduced. The most grievous aspect concerns the flourishing trade in zebra products. Whole zebra coats can be bought in shops in Nairobi for 600 dollars, handbags for eighty-five dollars and most insensate of all, covers for telephone directories for seventy-four dollars. There is also a lively export trade, especially in skins of the common zebra. In London, for example, a whole skin will fetch £400. The ban on hunting licences for shooting zebras is a welcome step—Kenya issued 63,000 licences in 1975 alone—but legal hunting is not the real danger. Poaching is always a menace where a lucrative trade can be pursued, and that is less easy to ban effectively. The Minister of Tourism and Wildlife in Kenya has declared that ninety-five per cent of all game trophies in the shops are legal—but, as has been pointed out, the ministry licenses the trophies for sale *after* they have been obtained by the shop owners!

A handsome pair of Burchell's zebra. Although they share territory with Grévy's there is no interbreeding

Cheetah: *diminishing prey for this 'big cat'*

The fastest land animal in the world, it is claimed, is the cheetah, although the pronghorn must run it very close. The cheetah has been used for centuries for sport by kings and maharajas and today is extinct, or virtually so, in the Indian subcontinent, although the scarcity of native cheetahs has brought about the importation of hunting animals from Africa. It still exists in southwest Asia, and about 200 are protected in reserves in Iran. The main stronghold of this speedy 'big cat' is Africa and even there the omens are far from reassuring and it is feared that even these numbers are dwindling fast.

Drastically reduced numbers

Formerly the cheetah ranged over the whole of Africa, with the exception of the Sahara and the tropical rain forests and apart from the southern parts of South Africa, it still does, but its numbers are much reduced. Thus, although cheetahs are to be found today in most of their

Right: a cheetah with a springbok it has killed. One reason for falling numbers of cheetahs in Africa is a decline in its prey species. Because it tends to opt for small animals it needs to kill more frequently than other 'big cats' and is often robbed of its prey. A more delicate balance exists between prey and predator than is the case with other related animals

Below: a modern perch

original regions they are thin on the ground and in whole areas in which they were formerly commonplace, they have disappeared. In Zaire, for example, Jacques Verschuren, the Belgian zoologist and authority on Zairian wildlife, reports that it is probable, but not certain, that it exists in small areas, but that the main place where it exists in significant numbers is on the high plateaux of the Kundelungu National Park. It so happens that it is there that an extraordinary abundance of oribis, the medium-sized antelope, is found and this gives a clue to one of the reasons for the decline of the cheetah in Africa—the falling numbers of prey species available to the animal.

Good market for cubs

In Ethiopia, a country at present in turmoil and which has been unstable for many years, the pressures on the cheetah are even better exemplified. Norman Myers has found that although still widespread its total numbers, even where it can be described as abundant, are far fewer than they were ten years ago. Here, also, the reduction in the prey species is a primary factor, but there are others. New roads have opened up the country giving the sport hunters more ready access to the haunts of the cheetah, the skins of which find a ready market.

Tiring cubs

To the normal high mortality among the cubs is added another hazard; they fetch a high price in European markets and are easily caught, the local tribesmen merely following a family party until one or more cubs tire and

A splendid view over the vast expanse of open space at Serengeti. Cheetahs like to sit high up to watch for prey

lag behind. A hundred a year may find their way to Europe and many die on the way. The unsettled times make control of the reserves and parks difficult and law enforcement nearly impossible. Finally, there are guerrillas anxious to sell trophies of all kinds for money in order to purchase arms and various weapons.

Natural pressures

In other countries farther south, where the typical habitat, the open savannah, is the rule, the natural pressures can be seen more clearly. In Uganda, Kenya and Tanzania, Myers declares that the cheetah could well be in a fair degree of trouble already 'from accelerating pressures'. These include being harried by large predators such as lions, leopards and hunting dogs and by scavengers (hyenas) and high cub mortality is inevitable from all these. The cubs are also prone to disease. A cheetah tends to kill small prey so it needs to kill more often than a leopard, for example. And frequently it so happens that cheetahs are robbed of their prey by others.

Sparse population

A recent estimate puts the number of cheetahs in Africa at 10,000 and possibly no more than 7000. This may seem an adequate enough figure from a conservation viewpoint until we remember that Africa possesses an area of twelve million square miles and the cheetah's range occupies at least half this figure. Even 10,000 scattered over the cheetah's range means that there is on average only one individual in every 600 square miles.

Cheetah skins on prominent display at a tourist souvenir stall in a market in Kano, northern Nigeria

Giant sable: *the twilight of a magnificent antelope*

It is somewhat ironic that the giant sable, which has been described as probably the most beautiful animal in the world, should have been unknown to science until 1916. This is not to say that its existence was unknown until then. The people of its native land, Angola, must have been aware of it and so must at least a few Europeans. The phrase 'known to science' indicates the moment when a full description of it has been published so that its existence is made known beyond doubt and a scientific name given.

Doubtful identity

Except that it has received a name, which removes it by definition from the category of being anonymous, anonymity has been and to a large extent still is the lot of this magnificent antelope. When, in 1909, the young Belgian engineer, H. F. Varian, employed by the Benguela Railway Company, reported what he had seen to the British Museum, strong doubts were expressed as to whether the animal was more than an unusual form of the sable antelope, an animal 'officially' named in 1838, but reported much earlier and ranging over a large part of subsaharan Africa. Then, in 1916, Oldfield Thomas was able to report to the Zoological Society of London that Varian had sent, from the Luando river area of Angola, a male scalp, frontlet and horns and a female mask and horns. These set the matter beyond doubt, and the recognition was reinforced in 1918, when several complete specimens were supplied to the Museum by a London zoologist, Gilbert Blaine.

Giant curving horns

The word 'sable' is medieval English for black and is in familiar use in heraldry to denote this colour. It is better known as the vernacular name for a small fur-bearing animal of the northern hemisphere, belonging to the weasel family, whose fur, incidentally, is brown. When, as almost invariably happens, the antelope is referred to as the giant sable there tends to be slight but temporary confusion. The adjective 'giant' can also be misleading, for the giant sable antelope is only slightly larger in the body than the much more common sable antelope. The use of the adjective is prompted by the great size of the magnificent sweeping horns, which curve up, back and down from the forehead, reaching a length of five feet on the curve, the record being sixty-five inches, with the tips almost touching the back.

The anonymity is emphasized in the words of David L. Niddre, one of the few to have photographed the beast in the wild, writing in *Animals*, 1970, 'No zoo in the world possesses one. Very few museums have a mounted specimen or group on display, though a scalp, face, and pair of horns adorn the walls of some men's clubs, great houses, and even modest farmhouses in southern Africa. A mere fifty or so lucky people will have an opportunity in any one year to observe a herd, and are just as likely to search for days without success'. Presumably Niddre is overlooking the local inhabitants of the reserve, to which the giant sable antelope is confined.

To begin with the antelope was killed for its meat and hide until the heyday of big game hunting, when the conspicuous arc of the horns represented an irresistible lure for the trophy hunter. These horns were the antelope's downfall, for they commanded a high price, for which not only the hunter with his rifle but also the local Africans (using assegae and pitfall traps) joined in the slaughter.

A male sable antelope, its dark colour set off dramatically against the light-coloured foliage of the African bush. There is very little obvious difference between the sable antelope and the giant sable. The 'giant' is only slightly larger in body size, but its horns are considerably bigger, sweeping over and at times almost touching the beast's back

The slaughter caused enlightened sportsmen to bring pressure to bear on the Angolan government, who in 1926 enacted a law making it illegal to kill the antelope except under special licence issued by the High Commissioner. The legislation was speeded by the Vernay Expedition of 1925, sponsored by the American Museum of Natural History, which brought back fifteen specimens for display there. After that permission to collect was hard to obtain, as several Europeans found. The Comte de Yebes was given permission to shoot two, one for himself and one for the Natural Science Museum in Madrid. Such was the rigour with which the law was enforced that it was not unknown for permission to shoot, obtained from the President of Portugal, being revoked by the colonial authorities in Luanda, the capital of Angola.

No figures exist, not surprisingly, for the former numbers of the giant sable antelope, living in the stretch of inaccessible light woodland lying between the Luando and Cuanza rivers. The antelope's ability to disappear into the scrub would have made counting almost impossible without a well-organized and numerically strong team working over an extended period of time, and this would probably have done more harm than good. *The Red Book of Wildlife in Danger*, 1969, gave the figure then of possibly 500 to 700 animals surviving.

Unfortunately, the law merely forbade killing and placed no embargo on the sale of trophies, so it was effective only against the sportsman, not the poacher. The local residents, therefore, pursued a lucrative but illicit trade in the bulls' trophies as well as killing the cows for their meat and hides. Secretly, traders offered potential buyers as many pairs of horns as they wished. (The African hunters supplying the trophies were likely to receive

An old photograph of a giant sable antelope (very likely a stuffed museum piece), showing the enormous expanse of the horns. It has been described as probably the most beautiful animal in the world, but was unknown to science until 1916

only a few cents for each one!) P. N. Gray stated in 1933 that he had heard several Portuguese brag of killing ten sables in a month. He also gave it as his opinion that this magnificent animal would soon be extinct, as no doubt it would have been but for the persistence of interested conservationists. One result of their dedication was that at the London conference for the protection of the flora and fauna of Africa, of 1933, the giant sable antelope was placed on the A-class list of species to be protected. Then, in 1934, a regulation published in Luanda recognized the need for a special reserve and a ban was placed on hunting.

Official forest reserve

Matters were not allowed to rest. The Luando Reserve was more closely defined by further regulations in 1937, 1938 and again in 1944. By a regulation of 1954, the Reserve was declared a forest reserve of two and a half million acres and a further separate reserve was declared to the north of the main reserve in 1963. Meanwhile, Bartolomeu Correia, farmer and businessman, as well as hunter, was invited to carry out a census, study the antelope's movements and list the African settlements within the reserve, with their then population of 12,000, as well as the names of licensed hunters. African game wardens were recruited. Indeed, everything possible that could be done at government level was carried out and the Portuguese government in Angola have long had the reputation for zealous application to the task of preserving an animal noted for its beauty as well as its rarity.

Impressive beauty of the herd

A giant sable antelope, especially a full-grown bull, stuffed, mounted and displayed in a museum is imposing. One living in a zoo, if that were possible, would be impressive. But the full beauty can only be seen when a small herd of them is seen free and in the wild, if we may judge by the graphic description given by Niddre, '. . . a mature bull—pitch black with a lighter underside and two incongruous white-circled eyes like a muse's mask. As he turns, you see the round white posterior bisected by the dark tasselled tail. The massive curving horns balanced so delicately upon a smallish head mesmerize you. . . . Over the low ridge the sun pours in a quiet yellow glow which gradually envelops the herd in front of you. The sitting animals have a wonderful dignity. As the light improves it is possible to see the concentric rings on the horns, the sharp tips, and even the soft wetness of the muzzles. The colours of the younger bucks show up as a bronze brown, while those of the mature animals are a sleeker, darker black with white contrasts. The leader of the herd seems almost conscious of his profile against the rising sun . . .'.

Conservation problems

So speaks one who has made the long and trying journey just to see this evanescent beauty before the antelopes drift away into the denser forest. But does the local person have the same aesthetic appreciation? The human population has risen to 18,000 or more, each family being forced to eke out a precarious living, cutting wood for building and burning and so reducing the habitat, clearing the ground of scrub to grow crops, which the antelopes may on occasion trample and browse. The animal itself represents meat, its sleek coat a desirable hide—and laws can be evaded. Moreover, there are no laws against cutting and burning. On top of this the political situation now is such that little consideration can be given effectively to conservation. So the opinion grows that the subspecies is bound to become extinct in the not too distant future unless the human population is removed and resettled on land outside the reserves. This must surely be an unacceptable solution.

Left: this group of sable antelopes, including a fully grown male and a group of young, gives an idea of the magnificence of a herd as described by Niddre

EXPLOITATION FOR THE FUR TRADE

Otter   Vicuña   Tiger   Leopard   Seal

Man has been clothing himself with furs since he learned to make the tools needed to do the skinning. The use of animal skins in this way was necessary when temperate and polar regions were first colonized, but the fur trade developed over the course of centuries until, by the middle of the twentieth century, exploitation had reached crazy proportions.

Eventually a chorus of protest built up against the use of animal furs and it reached its crescendo when fashion went mad. It seemed that the object of every woman's desire was a coat made from seal skin, chinchilla, or even leopard or tiger. Movements to wean the public from wearing furs grew up and these were reinforced by technological advances in making synthetic furs, which are almost indistinguishable from the real thing and much cheaper, too.

1970 became something of a landmark in the history of conservation, when the International Fur Trade Federation (IFTF) and the International Union for the Conservation of Nature and Natural Resources (IUCN) began having discussions. As a result the IFTF recommended a total ban on trade in the skins of five gravely endangered animals and a temporary ban on two more. In addition the IFTF expressed a willingness to participate in a joint survey with the Survival Service Commission of the IUCN of the jaguar, ocelot and margay. The United States already had its Endangered Species Act and the Lacey Act became a model in legislation for other countries to follow.

This section discusses efforts made in recent years to protect fur-bearing animals from the demands of the fashion trade.

A group of Indian otters

Otter: *too-easy prey for the hunter*

When Nicole Duplaix-Hall described an otter as a seal with a long tail she gave us the most apt and succinct description of this aquatic animal. There are seven genera of otters involving eighteen species, although it is possible that some of the five species of South American river otters will eventually prove to be no more than subspecies. This would reduce slightly the number of species. The eighteen species, as recognized at present, represent the most widely distributed of all groups of mammals. They are worldwide except for the Arctic regions, Antarctica, Australasia and Malagasy. Before mankind became so widespread, and indeed until early historical times, there were otters in every river and stream, except for the areas mentioned. In addition, there was a sea otter in the coastal waters of the whole of the North Pacific and another along the Pacific seaboard of South America, the marine otter.

Fine waterproof fur

Wherever they are found, and to whatever species they belong, otters are much alike. They differ mainly in size and in small details of anatomy, and with the exception of the sea otter, which seldom comes on land, they are similar in habit. One of the physical adaptations of otters to their aquatic life is the possession of a fine waterproof fur and this is their undoing. Except for the giant Brazilian otter, they are largely nocturnal and they

certainly quickly become strictly nocturnal when disturbed by the persistent presence of humans. This, with their extreme agility in water and general elusiveness, should have given them security. Nobody would have troubled to hunt them systematically without the prospect of a rich reward from their fur, although it has to be admitted that in England, and possibly to a lesser extent elsewhere, otter-hunting, using a pack of hounds, has long been a favourite sport and has been favoured because of the challenge provoked by the very elusiveness of the quarry.

Vulnerable to man

Other things apart, the otter has been vulnerable to the human presence from very early times, simply because it seeks its food in water. Rivers have long served as highways for people, in everyday life, in primitive commerce, in fishing and in opening up new territories. Rivers and streams are the easiest means of access through forests and jungles. So man and otter confronted each other early on and once the confrontation proved lucrative it continued even after the rivers had ceased to be the main means of day-to-day travel.

Otters can easily be tamed and keeping them as pets has been popular and has been another drain on numbers in the wild. In southeast Asia, from China and the Himalayas through to Borneo, fishermen have tamed the small-clawed otter to assist in catching fish, training them to bring the fish to hand.

While otter fur proved a valuable marketable commodity, the pelt has other uses and although these subsidiary interests did not make wholesale impact they speeded up the decline in otter populations everywhere.

In South America, among the aboriginal peoples, otter pelts have long been a ready source for leather. In Africa, among certain tribes, only a tribal chief was allowed to wear otter fur and offenders were fined an ox, which was certainly a heavy fine. This would have restricted otter-hunting to some extent, but otter fur was also the sovereign remedy for a stiff neck, with no penalty for merely applying a fur to the neck.

A Canadian trapper and his family. Because of the demand for skins for fur coats a tremendous amount of trapping occurs in Canada

The widespread use of the fur commercially, especially for coat collars and trimmings was, however, the main cause for the decline in numbers and the greatness of its impact is well illustrated by the sea otter. Within historic times the sea otter ranged, in good numbers, from Lower California northwards, through the Aleutians and the Kurile and Commander islands and along the coast of Kamchatka, Asia. Sea-otter skins have been the most expensive of all furs and were often used by royalty. This brought the species to the verge of extinction, which was averted only by rigorous protective measures.

Impact of the fur trade

To a greater or lesser degree, it is the same story for otters throughout their wide range. An exception is the African clawless otter, the fur of which is not so desirable as that of other otters and it has consequently not been extensively hunted. Nevertheless, as in the case of other otters disturbance and change in the habitat, with expanding human populations, have been harmful to it. It cannot be too strongly emphasized, however, that it is the fur trade that has made the greatest impact on otters and deterioration of the habitat has only been a very poor second, with possibly one exception, the South American southern river otter.

In England the reason given for sustaining the persecution of otters by hunting them as a sport has been that they are the enemy of the angler. This may be an excuse rather than a reason, since despite the otter's agility in water, it tends to take only sickly or weak fish and also eels, which are beyond doubt the main competitors of the sport fisherman. The southern river otter is slightly less speedy than the Eurasian otter. There have been introduced into its habitat quantities of trout, which not only feed on the slower native fish but can, it is said, evade the otter. That at least is the theory, although it is suspected that the fishermen coming to catch the trout also disturb the habitat, to the detriment of the otter.

Shot in groups

Probably the most vulnerable of all otters, after the sea otter, is the giant Brazilian otter, because it is steadfastly diurnal, whereas other species are only nocturnal or become mainly so when men disturb the habitat. Another feature of its behaviour that threatens its security is that it is gregarious. It is usually found in groups of four to six, but sometimes as many as fifteen. It sleeps in groups on steep river banks and hauls out at favourite feeding places, where the remains of meals lead the hunter to watch for it. Trapping is not necessary. It can be shot and groups are slaughtered while asleep.

Found in the north Pacific the sea otter lives in groups on remote coasts, feeding on sea urchins, mollusks, crabs, fish and seaweed

The figures for the export of giant otter pelts from Peru, through which the skins were traded, tell their own tale. In 1947 2248 skins were exported. Since then there has been a more or less steady decline until 1971, when only twelve skins were exported and there has been no export since. This happened without protective measures or government legislation. Scientists who have travelled through the areas where otters should be found have reported seeing none in the main streams of the Amazon basin and only the occasional one in the remoter reaches. R. A. Mittermeier regards the giant otter as the most endangered Amazonian mammal. There are predictions that the species could be extinct within a decade, although, on the optimistic side, it is protected in Peru, and in Surinam it is not only protected but the fur trade is not well developed.

Gloomy predictions

The giant otter is not alone as the subject of gloomy predictions. The marine otter of the Pacific coast of South America and the southern river otter have both been added to the Red Data Book of endangered species. The smooth-coated Indian otter was said, in 1973, to have reached the remnant stage and to be in immediate danger of extinction unless protected. In the same year the spotted-necked otter of Africa was also said to be in grave danger of extinction.

It is only when an experienced naturalist makes a survey of a given region that such pronouncements are made and it is necessary to wait for further visits, which are at best infrequent, to know whether the position

The common otter is the species which occurs in Britain. It weighs up to about thirty-three pounds and feeds on crayfish, fish, frogs and small aquatic birds

has improved or worsened. Consequently, the status of any particular species is difficult to assess at any given moment. With few exceptions otters are elusive. Usually the most one sees is footprints in mud, spraints (droppings) and remains of meals. Where these are fresh all that can be said is that an otter passed that way recently, a guide that is not conducive to giving exact numbers present in the whole area. Even in a heavily settled area, such as England, where in recent years attention has been focused intensively on the native otter, with many naturalists keeping watch, no precise data can be given. All that can be said, and that in general terms only, is that otters everywhere seem to be on the decline and that only through the fur trade and the banning of exports internationally can the trend be reversed.

Misleading facts

In the absence of precise data gloomy forecasts could be misleading. Thus, alarm at what appeared to be a serious decrease in the number of native otters in Britain was sounded as recently as 1951 and there is still some doubt as to how serious the decline is. By contrast there is a sentence in the *National Encyclopedia*, published around 1900 (the volumes are undated) which reads: 'In England it (the common or Eurasian otter) is becoming very scarce, and is almost extinct except in a few counties.' Either there was a recovery in numbers in the intervening fifty years, followed by another drop nearer to the 1950s or we have a splendid example of the small value of generalizations unsupported by actual censuses.

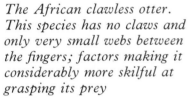

The African clawless otter. This species has no claws and only very small webs between the fingers; factors making it considerably more skilful at grasping its prey

More severely practical are the results from the protection of the sea otter. This animal lives in the kelp beds of the North Pacific and formerly ranged from Kamchatka to Lower California. Slaughter for its valuable fur in the eighteenth century brought it near to extinction. Protection in 1910 by the United States government, followed by other governments, saved the sea otter, which has steadily increased its range and its numbers, although slowly, until 1970. Progress has been reported since, although the species still occupies only one-fifth of its former range. It is, however, now back in waters off Lower California and in some places there has been a tenfold increase in numbers since protection was given. In 1971 the experiment was tried of transporting a score or so to British Columbia from Alaska and later to Oregon, to places where they used to live. In both places they are reported as having bred.

Keystone species

Another lesson is to be learned from the sea otter. The animal feeds largely on sea urchins, which when in large numbers ravage the kelp. By preying on these they save the kelp from being overgrazed, so saving the balance of nature from being upset. Among animals that benefit are harbor seals and bald eagles and possibly many others. That is, the sea otter is a keystone species, one that controls the welfare of a number of other species. For all we know to the contrary the river otters hold similar positions and their disappearance could be just as significant.

The extraordinary reddish colour of this giant otter is caused by the hue of the river bank soil of its habitat

Vicuña: *ruthless exploitation for its fine wool*

Before the Spaniards overthrew the Inca empire in 1532, there were more than a million vicuñas in the High Andes, the altiplano, of Peru. There were many more in the Andes of Bolivia, Chile and Argentina, but man's impact on the vicuña, a small member of the camel family, has been most intense in Peru, where the use of its wool for garments was forbidden, on pain of death, except to those of royal birth. The animals were rounded up in royal hunts in which thousands of beaters drove them into stone-walled corrals or into canyons or else formed a circle, which closed in on them. These were captured, shorn and released, except for aged or injured individuals, which were slaughtered, their meat being distributed among the beaters as a reward for the day's work. Although the species was exploited its conservation was ensured since the same area was worked only once in every four years.

The royal favour shown for the vicuña's coat was because its wool is without exception the finest to be obtained from any animal. It has been described as softer than that from the Cashmere goat and five times as valuable. Inevitably, the conquerors coveted such a product, but failed to appreciate the Inca's conservation methods. They hunted the vicuña with dogs and firearms, killing 80,000 a year throughout the rest of the sixteenth century, and the slaughter they began continued through succeeding centuries. The result was that by 1957 the vicuña population was down to 400,000. Worse was to come when in that year a sudden expanding market

With the help of its warm, thick coat the vicuña is able to withstand the harsh climate of its habitat, the Andes

Vicuña

developed for exported vicuña wool. The best overcoats in Dallas and Beverly Hills were made from the five tons of vicuña wool imported each year from Bolivia, representing 40,000 vicuñas. The animals were hunted mercilessly, the hunters using landrovers and helicopters and using such ruthless weapons as machine-guns. Even the water holes were poisoned in a slaughter even more barbaric than that of the early Spanish invaders. By 1968 the numbers had fallen dramatically to not more than 12,000, of which as few as 2000 ranged over Bolivia, Chile and Argentina.

Effective clampdown

In that year the decline of this small camelid was noted by the International Union for the Conservation of Nature (IUCN), who declared it an endangered species. A ten-year agreement was drawn up between Peru and Bolivia to ban all hunting, to prohibit the sale of vicuña wool and products and to generally protect the species. So rigidly was this adhered to that any wool harvested, whether from illegal sources, confiscated from poachers, or from legal sources, from ranches, research stations or reserves, was stored during this ten-year period to guard against illegally obtained wool being sold as legal. The clampdown was complete.

It is on record that the only exception was a vicuña wool poncho, a South American cloak, oblong in shape, with a slit in the middle for the head, which was presented to Fidel Castro by the government during his tour of Peru.

Following the example of Peru and Bolivia, in 1974 Chile and Argentina agreed to this ban. Moreover, a ban was placed on the export of live vicuñas except to zoos, and since most of these had up till now come from Argentina, that country's co-operation was important. In the meantime, both the United States and the United Kingdom banned the import of vicuña wool and vicuña products.

Wardens shot

As always, in spite of governments doing all they can to block up the loopholes, illegal trading, though becoming more difficult, continued in both wool and the live animals. Unfortunately, as long as there is a demand for any product there are always those who are prepared to transport it, buy and sell it, especially when the commodity commands a price fifty times that of sheep's wool. These illicit traders depend ultimately on poachers for supply and although the surviving vicuñas are in reserves, patrolling wardens have to work in tough country at personal risk. Angela West, in covering the subject, has recorded that in 1971 two wardens were shot and in 1974 a party of poachers, having just slaughtered eighty vicuñas, turned their guns on a party of guards, killing one and wounding two others.

Vicuña reserves

The very size of the reserves needed is another drawback. In 1966 the Peruvian government set aside 150,000 acres for the Pampa Galeras National Vicuña Reserve, 300 miles south of Lima. Bolivia followed, in 1972, with the National Fauna Reserve of Ulla Ulla, covering 500,000 acres and Chile created the million-acre Lauca National Park. Such parks not only serve to protect the vicuña but also other wildlife in the area. In 1976 a new reserve was created in Bolivia in somewhat different circumstances. The owner of a farm 13,000 feet up in the Andes, within easy reach of the town of La Paz, planted 7000 acres of alfalfa for Friesian cows to graze. The vicuñas came in to feed and the owner, Jorge Rodriguez Balanza, did not disturb them. Instead, he informed the Wildlife Department that 300 vicuñas were living on his land and the area was

Vicuñas usually stay close together, but will spread out if they have trouble finding enough food. The male protects the females, the young and the territory from other male intruders

declared a fauna reserve. Moreover, there was the hope that a larger area of land adjacent to it would be set aside to give room for any increase in the vicuña population. Figures for other reserves encourage this hope.

Making a comeback

Without a deliberate census being made over the whole range it is not possible to give up-to-date figures for a species. Where a species is given protection by several countries the dates for the latest estimates tend not to coincide and so the total populations at any given moment can only be crudely estimated. That the vicuña is still making a comeback can be gauged by the latest figures available. There are 40–50,000 in Peru, 2000 in Bolivia, 3000 in Chile and up to 10,000 in Argentina.

Extinction averted

The Incas protected it, the Spaniards slew it, successive governments in Peru and Bolivia, since the days of Simon Bolivar, have passed laws making it an offence to hunt, much less to kill the vicuña or to sell the fleece or cloth made from it, and contraband trading in the twentieth century threatened the animal with complete extinction—as happened to the chinchilla in the wild. The timely foundation of reserves, with which the name of Felipe Benivades must always be associated, averted this.

Although other members of the camel family—the Arabian and Bactrian camels, the llama, alpaca and guanaco—have all been successfully domesticated, the vicuña does not thrive in captivity. Instead, it becomes very prone to disease and deterioration, particularly in the coat, tends to set in. Banning exports, curbing poachers and providing large, secure reserves is, therefore, the only answer.

Tiger: *the fight against poaching*

Everyone knows the tiger, the largest and most handsome of the 'big cats', and prior to 1969 anyone would have thought that of all the animals in the world this one was best fitted to look after itself. Powerful, ferocious, a skilled hunter, the general impression would have been that the tiger was a menace to man, a man-eater. It came therefore as something of a shock to learn that this imperious beast had gone into rapid decline and that it was doubtful whether, if something drastic were not done, it would survive to the end of the twentieth century.

Threatened Bengal tiger

In December 1969, the Ninth General Assembly of the International Union for the Conservation of Nature and Natural Resources (IUCN) met in New Delhi and decided to add the Bengal tiger to the list of the world's most endangered species. In fact, the Bengal tiger is a subspecies of the tiger *Panthera tigris*, one of eight subspecies of which one, the Bali tiger, was then already extinct and six others were down to low numbers. The tiger as a species formerly ranged over most of Asia, from Siberia to the island of Bali in Indonesia and from Turkey and the Caspian Sea eastwards, including the whole of southern Asia. As recently as 1939 it was estimated that the population of the Bengal tiger, the most typical of the subspecies, numbered 30,000 in the whole of the Indian subcontinent alone. In 1969 the estimate was right down to a figure under 2000.

Right: unlike most of the other members of the cat family, tigers are not afraid of water and are strong swimmers. They are known to bathe in order to cool off in hot weather

Below: a scene from the past; big game in India

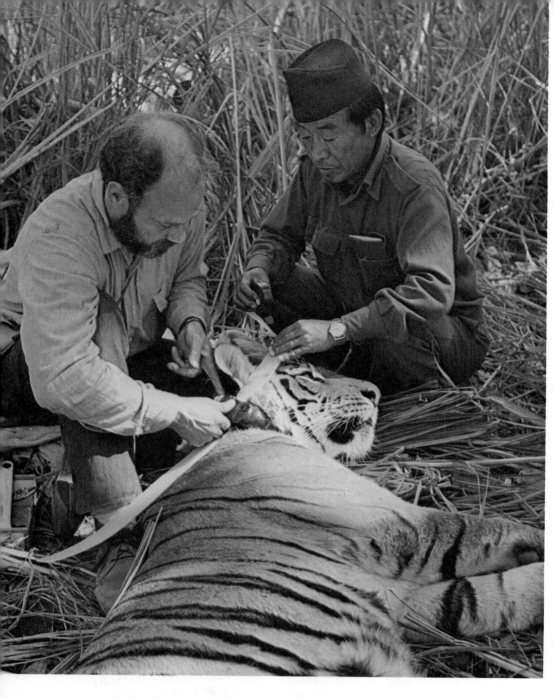

A drugged tigress is fitted with a radio collar in order to study her behavioural patterns: part of the project to save the tigers in the Royal Chitwan National Park, Nepal

At that time, the assessments for the subspecies were: the Siberian tiger from 120 to 130; the Sumatran tiger a few hundreds; the Chinese tiger very scarce; the Indo-Chinese tiger rapidly declining; the Caspian tiger with a maximum of fifty and the Javan tiger with a maximum of twelve. This noble animal, the hunting of which had for so long been the sport of kings and maharajas was on the decline everywhere. King George V of Great Britain and his party had, in 1912, shot thirty-nine tigers in eleven days and by 1965 one maharaja could boast of having shot 1150 tigers. It was not, as might be thought, the massive organized tiger-hunts in the days of the British Raj, particularly, that had brought about this dramatic decline, but a variety of circumstances of which a taste for tiger skin in fashion was among the most significant.

Tiger's range invaded

The main cause for the disappearance of the tiger was, however, the large and steady increase in the human population. This brought with it the spread of agriculture, virgin land converted to pasture, land reclamation, expansion of forestry plantations, new roads, new towns, extension of railways, new airports and new hydroelectric schemes. In addition, much of the tiger's range has been the scene of warfare, including defoliation of forests in southeast Asia. Even without actual fighting, war-like activities can be detrimental. In 1972 the build-up of troops on the Sino-Soviet

80

border took place in some of the best habitat for the Manchurian tiger and this proved unfavourable for the tiger. All these influences not only serve to decrease the effective area of habitat but reduce the numbers of the tiger's prey species, especially the deer and the wild cattle. Yet such things are inevitable in the march of human progress and the relentless, surreptitious, day-to-day poaching and hunting is probably far more damaging.

Poaching continues

Originally the killing of tigers other than in organized hunts (shikars) was for two purposes. One was based on the superstition that almost any part of the tiger had aphrodisiac properties and the other on the idea that eating the flesh gave the diner the strength of the animal. Hunting for these reasons probably still goes on, perhaps to a lesser extent. Today, and for a decade or so past, the day-to-day killing has been augmented by poaching for the fur trade, which in spite of official bans, still goes on.

Boom in trophy and coat trade

The real slaughter began when air travel became general, following the end of the Second World War and hunters from all over the world converged on Asia to secure prized trophies in the form of tiger-skin rugs and heads to hang on the wall. Simultaneously came sales promotions for tiger-skin coats with the result that prices soared. The hunters, in the course of a twenty-day shikar, were prepared to pay well for an official licence to kill one tiger, merely to have the skin, which might cost up to 10,000 dollars, and head, as trophies of the hunt. Those organizing the shikars could, by unscrupulous and surreptitious means, make it possible, on receipt of a suitable bribe for their connivance, for two or three tigers to be shot on the one licence. For skins intended for the fur trade 2000 dollars was the usual price and the local poacher would receive 100 dollars, a fortune for a member of an impoverished population.

At this same time, under the Foreign Aid programme, Asian governments were receiving large quantities of pesticides, including dieldrin and later folidol, for agricultural purposes. It was soon discovered that a carcase of a goat laced with poisonous pesticide and

Below right: Tara, a tiger born in Twycross Zoo, England, was shipped to India and presented for a privately funded project to rehabilitate zoo-born 'big cats' for the wild

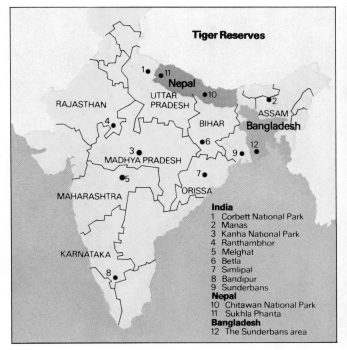

Tiger Reserves

RAJASTHAN
Nepal
UTTAR PRADESH
ASSAM
Bangladesh
BIHAR
MADHYA PRADESH
ORISSA
MAHARASHTRA
KARNATAKA

India
1 Corbett National Park
2 Manas
3 Kanha National Park
4 Ranthambhor
5 Melghat
6 Betla
7 Simlipal
8 Bandipur
9 Sunderbans
Nepal
10 Chitawan National Park
11 Sukhla Phanta
Bangladesh
12 The Sunderbans area

placed in tiger country was an effective means of securing a skin plus its head, both easy to sell on the black market. Tigers that were not poisoned were still at risk from the more affluent, but still illegal, hunters who worked by night with a jeep, a spotlight and a rifle.

'Project Tiger'

Such was the situation when the Ninth General Assembly of IUCN met in New Delhi in December 1969. India responded by putting an embargo on the export of skins. So did Pakistan and other governments soon followed. It was an expression of intent, but the practical result was to drive the illegal trade underground. With long coastlines, numerous ports, cargo ships in harbour with crew members ready to be bribed and room in the ships to hide a few salted skins, the products of poaching slipped past even the most zealous customs officials. However, a plan to save the tiger was under way. Saving it had become a multi-national co-operative and on April 1 1973, at the Corbett National Park, north of Delhi, 'Project Tiger' was launched, which had the enthusiastic support of the then prime minister, Mrs Indira Ghandi. The scheme was to last until March 1979 and was to have an initial budget of eight million dollars, an eighth of which was to come from the World Wildlife Fund. It was not possible for the Federal Government to order the necessary action, but by 1970 all states of the Indian Union had already declared tiger-hunting illegal. Nepal and Bangladesh had followed in 1971.

Not only was hunting made illegal but the chief wildlife warden, or officers authorized by him, had powers to control skins, trophies and products already in store and to mark them so that they could later be identified. It was also made illegal to sell a skin. In addition, plans were put forward to establish reserves that would support viable populations of tigers. The ideal reserves would be large areas of 800 square miles arranged in adjoining blocks in which periodic culling could take place and

The tiger's striped coat serves as splendid camouflage in the dappled light of the jungle

in which there could be ordered intermingling to safeguard a genetic pool and so avoid inbreeding. In a country with a rapidly expanding population it would be impracticable to set aside such vast areas of land, so it was decided to designate eight areas (see map), each of which would have the potential for developing its viable population.

Two other aims would be envisaged. First, such areas would also help to preserve other wildlife within their boundaries. Secondly, and seldom far from any wildlife preservation scheme, is the possibility of attracting tourism.

Project deserves success

In any well-laid conservation plan the chances of 100 per cent success are remote and reports since 1973 suggest that loopholes for illicit trading in tiger skins still exist and that this trading still goes on. At least 'Project Tiger' deserves success. Some idea of how far it is succeeding can be gained from scattered reports received since 1973. Thus, although tiger-hunting was not prohibited in Malaya, as it was in neighbouring countries, the Malayan Ministry of Agriculture decided not to issue further licences and to intensify its campaign against trapping tigers and other wild animals. Almost simultaneously came the report that in the Maritime Territory of the Soviet Far East a census had shown between 110 and 120 tigers, a three to fourfold increase since the 1940s, thanks to effective protection. Moreover, the tigers there seemed to be adapting to life near human settlements although still avoiding people.

In 1976 a tiger in Bangladesh killed a woman and instead of being killed it was translocated to a reserve after being captured with anaesthetic darts, action that gives an idea of the prompt response to the movement to preserve tigers. This had, however, an unexpected sequel. The erring tiger was later found dead, killed no doubt for territorial reasons by other tigers already in the reserve. This illustrates one of the obstacles to moving wild

Hardly a camouflage in these surroundings, the tigers' coats contrast strikingly with the snow

Described as 'fun furs' in 1967, these amazingly extravagant outfits are now fortunately a thing of the past

animals into reserves: the possibility that established occupants will not be too happy to accept newcomers.

In 1977 there were only five remaining tigers in the Meru Betiri reserve in Java, which is almost the last remaining reserve. In the island as a whole tigers are now very rare. In the same year Markus Borner said that he thought that the Sumatran tiger could become extinct fairly soon. He estimated that there were 800 left, with very few in nature reserves, and that they were being poached at a rate of 100 a year. By contrast it was reported that tigers had increased in the demilitarized zone in Korea, where nobody may go without a permit! The latest report for India says that tigers are increasing there.

Leopard: *victim of cruelty*

More concern seems to have been felt about the leopard than the other spotted cats, but there is a measure of disagreement about exactly how far its survival as a species is threatened as well as to what extent the animal conflicts with human interests.

Taking the question of survival first, there is a comprehensive report on the large spotted cats in Africa by Dr Norman Myers, who undertook a survey in 1972 for the International Union for the Conservation of Nature and Natural Resources (IUCN) and the World Wildlife Fund International. He also produced a report on the cheetah in the following year. His conclusion was that the leopard was in much better shape than the cheetah because it is of a solitary, secretive and nocturnal nature and therefore keeps more out of sight. It is also more secure because it can adapt to almost any habitat, from semi-desert through grassland scrub to lowland and mountain forest. It is at home in the dense rain forest and also can accommodate to human disturbance. Moreover, it can adapt its prey to circumstances, turning to an alternative prey species if its usual one becomes rare. In one area its main prey may be impala, in another the hyrax. Consequently, the leopard seems well equipped to withstand the

A leopard lying on a branch in a park in Sri Lanka. Smaller in build than the other 'big cats', they are far more agile

pressures due to increasing human settlement, provided that circumstances are not especially adverse.

The leopard is, pound for pound, the strongest of all the 'big cats' and can hold its own, unlike the cheetah, which suffers in physical competition with other predators of about its own size. A typical example of this is the conflict between lion and leopard. The lion is the bigger and has not infrequently been observed trying to rob a leopard of its kill. The leopard usually thwarts it by carrying its prey (sometimes almost equal to its own weight) up into a tree, where the lion cannot follow, and caching it over a branch or in a fork.

Myers' study

The leopard formerly ranged throughout Africa and southern Asia, except in the deserts. Myers' study was restricted to subsaharan Africa. He found that entire tracts of Kenya, Somalia, Ethiopia, Nigeria, Zambia, Rhodesia, Namibia and other countries had been almost completely cleared of leopards within the past few years. South Africa has shown that seventy-five per cent of leopards can be eliminated in a relatively short space of time, leaving just a remnant in reserves and national parks or in mountains, deserts and environments that are too arid to be of interest to humans. In the Kruger Park, for example, where there are numerous impala, there is no shortage of leopards. In the Aberdare forest of Kenya, on the other hand, Myers found a density of one leopard for every square mile and the same for the Rhodes Matapos Park in Rhodesia. In the Zaire river basin Myers estimated that there must be over 100,000 leopards, but unlike other areas poaching is virtually non-existent there.

Above: expert climbers,
leopards spend a great deal of
time in trees

Left: two young African
leopards crouching in the fork
of a tree

In the Miombo woodland zone, covering much of Zambia, Mozambique and Angola, as well as southern Tanzania, substantial numbers of leopards still exist in spite of extensive poaching.

Patchy distribution

Scattered reports from other authors in other areas of Africa show a similar patchy distribution, but leopards are less numerous. In Ghana, where they used to be common, there were only occasional sightings in 1970 and only three sightings in 1975. In Sierra Leone, where formerly they were frequent, they were reported to be seldom seen in 1971. In Nigeria, in the National Park W, they were reported in 1973 also to be seldom seen. In Morocco and Algeria, during these same years, they were reported to be 'still present', although presumably not in great numbers, while in Egypt they were said to be rare. In 1973, leopards were said to be numerous in many areas, with what seems to be the typical density of one per square mile, while in other areas they were decreasing. Significantly, however, several reports indicate that more leopard skins are being exported from Ethiopia than ever before, and this in spite of the International Fur Trade Federation (IFTF) ban.

In southern Asia, the other part of the leopard's range, the situation seems to be similar. In Turkey it was estimated, in 1974, that there were no more than ten pairs left. In Israel, for 1975, there were said to be very few remaining. In Iran for these same years the species was apparently holding its own adequately.

The overall situation can be summed up as follows. Over the continent of Africa a hundred years ago the species was abundantly and evenly distributed almost everywhere, except for the coastal Mediterranean strip and parts of South Africa. Now the leopard's numbers are decreasing and in some areas it has been virtually eliminated. In a few areas, such as the huge rain forest of Zaire, the status quo has been maintained. In smaller areas, such as national parks and reserves, and also in places like the Aberdare forest of Kenya, the same satisfactory situation prevails. Elsewhere, as Myers puts it, there is for the most part one leopard where formerly there were twenty and where ten could now exist without undue conflict with human interests. Therefore, the kind of situation has been achieved naturally that would have been reached anyway if only certain additional areas had been designated as reserves.

Attitudes of local people

The question is, then, how far can this position be maintained in the future? The answer to this depends on the attitude of local residents, and this in turn depends on the twin factors: how far can the presence of leopards be tolerated and to what extent will the fur trade remain lucrative? Put another way, the attitude of the local peoples depends not only on whether the animal is a menace to themselves and their livestock but whether poaching for the fur trade remains worth while.

The question of conflict of human interests, as has been said, is divided,

Below left: leopards often wedge food remains in a tree to protect them from scavengers

Bottom left: leopards feed on antelopes, baboons, monkeys, hyraxes and large rodents

and for suitable illustration of this we turn to a report in a South African newspaper for 1970. In a congress of Cape Divisional Councils a motion was put forward seeking to reintroduce bounties on leopard skins. Those supporting the motion argued that numbers of the leopard were increasing and heavy damage was being sustained among livestock. One instance quoted was of a farmer who lost sixty head of stock in one night and his neighbours, it was claimed, lost even more. This seems a heavy loss for a beast that 'stalks alone', but it may possibly have been a case of a solitary 'rogue' individual. Conservationists present argued that leopards were becoming fewer in number, even approaching extinction in some districts.

Benefit to farmer

It is even arguable as to whether leopards are normally a menace. One South African farmer, speaking in another context, has recorded that he had leopards on his farm that were of considerable benefit. They not only left his livestock unmolested and caused no menace to people living on the farm but even preyed on animals that were invading the farm to feed on

What has been said in this article about the leopard could equally be said of the jaguar. There is a brisk traffic in illicit skins and poaching is done by trap and other gruesome methods

vegetable crops. This story echoes accounts published elsewhere. In Sierra Leone, where leopards have been almost wiped out, the grey vervet monkey has proliferated at an alarming rate, invading cultivated fields and seriously damaging crops. In Somalia, where leopards had been much reduced, warthogs and other vegetable-eaters increased greatly in number and ravaged the crops.

The best remedy in this situation seems to be the controlled killing of rogue individuals that are a nuisance, rather than a general campaign against the species as a whole. Unrestricted killing has several drawbacks. Too often it leads to unwarranted cruelty. Inexpert marksmen inflict fatal wounds, the animal escaping to die an agonizing death. Traps and poisons are even worse. One of the more ingenious and cruel traps on record is made by burying a lance, with a poisoned tip, vertically in the ground with only its point above the surface. A freshly killed baboon is then hung above it just out of reach. The leopard jumps to claw down the carcase and then falls back on to the lance to die a slow, lingering death. The more common method is, however, by straightforward poisoning. A leopard will eat carrion readily and it is all too easy to poison meat and lay it out for the beast to take. Death by poison, too, invariably leads to painful death.

Money lure

Another drawback to unrestricted killing, which normally means poaching, is that it may lead to other even more rare species in the neighbourhood being slaughtered. Once a poacher has obtained a leopard skin and sold it through an illicit channel, the prospect of relatively easy money lures him to further killings. He may then learn that other trophies have a marketable value, to collectors, and these may come from species as yet not protected, although they may be rare.

The moral of this story is that the most effective remedy for the demise of both leopard and jaguar would be to dissuade people from using the skins in any way. If either of these spotted animals were to become extinct the culprits could quite safely be named—those who pay a high price for skins, whether they are used for the purposes of fashion or as trophies.

It is believed that the jaguar could become extinct by 1980 in Mexico and Argentina, where its habitat has been destroyed. Only about 100 remained when a count was made in 1972. Because jaguars are scarce their skins command a high price

Seal: *a grim traffic in skins*

Conservation may be defined in a variety of ways. A slightly cynical definition could be that it is an attempt by a small minority to protect actively and systematically part of the world's wildlife from the destructive activities of another small minority, with the bulk of the people ranged on the sidelines either decidely neutral (or apathetic) or at best merely cheering on their chosen side. This picture, something very like a global football match, is enhanced by the way emotions are aroused and tempers inflamed with the chance always in the offing of a little hooliganism or vandalism.

Orkney sanctuary

Grey seal pups are born with a cream woolly coat, which is replaced after three weeks by a blue-grey sea-going one. Fed on fat-rich milk, the pups grow rapidly after birth and put on up to fifty pounds in weight, most of which consists of blubber, in two weeks

Generalization tends to obscure details. In this case no notice is taken of the many, who quietly and unobtrusively try by individual effort to establish local sanctuaries for harassed wildlife. Some years ago, for example, an organization, the Ferne Trust, bought a remote island in the Orkney group as a sanctuary for the grey seal. The hope was that the seals would come to recognize it as a safe place and stay there. The seals off Norway, for example, were slaughtered for food for ranched silver foxes and their numbers declined more than could be accounted for by the slaughter. At the same time the numbers of seals on the coasts of Britain

increased. Then there were unusual disturbances to seals off Britain and the numbers of seals off Norway correspondingly increased rapidly.

Mediterranean monk seals are protected in some places, persecuted elsewhere. They are shot by fishermen in some places because of the traditional idea that they are harmful to fisheries. (In one place in Italy where vineyards come down to the sea, seals are accused of damaging the grape crops and therefore shot.) Where persecuted it is noticeable that the seals retreat to caves, offshore islands or beaches at the foot of precipitous cliffs. So the Ferne Trust was not wholly misguided in attempting to create a sanctuary in Orkney.

Hunted from early times

In the early years of human history the seas must have been teeming with seals everywhere. Every part of seals' anatomy suggests that their ancestors were land carnivores, related to wolves and dogs. In taking to water they found a rich food supply in the form of fish, as well as security from enemies and freedom from competitors. As man spread across the world their paradise became eroded. Man has hunted seals from very early times, but with the upsurge of maritime exploration in the fifteenth and sixteenth centuries came systematic sealing. As the centuries passed, sealing became heavier. It was a lucrative trade carried on by tough men to supply their land-based fellows with warm clothing. One species of seal after another became reduced in numbers, some to the verge of extinction. As one sealing ground became uneconomic another was sought, even in

A huge poster that was erected by the Fund for Animal Welfare opposite Canada House, Trafalgar Square, London, protesting against the barbarous springtime seal hunt off the Newfoundland coast

Northern fur seals from the world's largest herd of mammals. They come ashore to breed on two islands in the Pribilof group in the north Pacific. Despite the annual cull the population is stable

the distant and, furthermore, extremely inhospitable waters of the Antarctic.

If the story of sealing were given in full it would contain heart-rending stories of cruelty, of inefficient death blows, of lingering deaths, of seals skinned while their hearts were still beating. Towards the end of the nineteenth century the consciences of some individuals, even of a few governments, began to be uneasy, mainly perhaps from the realization that if things continued in the same way the time would come when the harvest of furs would be so slender as to be not worth taking. Not all seals carry valuable furs. There are those known specifically as the fur seals, which carry an extra-rich fur. They, more particularly, were the targets of the sealing industry. Others, with less-valuable furs, were the victims more of indiscriminate hunting in the supposed interests of fisheries.

Protection in the Baltic

In the Baltic today seals are protected by some countries bordering this inland sea, and this protection is largely the result of governments withdrawing bounties on seals. Finland is an outstanding exception. Its government seems to have refused to withdraw bounties as a result of pressure from commercial fisheries' interests. Elsewhere in the world conservation schemes have been put into effect checking the decline in seal populations and of these the story of the Pribilof fur seals is a textbook example.

The Pribilof islands lie off the coast of Alaska. The Pribilof, Alaskan, or Northern fur seal uses them as breeding grounds. Outside the breeding season the fur seals disperse over the northern Pacific. These seals numbered several million before the sealers set upon them. By 1911 their numbers were reduced to a dangerously low level, and through international agreement the Pribilof islands were put under strict control. The annual catch was limited. Then, by a brilliant stroke, American biologists suggested that this annual catch should be confined to superfluous bachelor males, that is, those not yet old enough to breed, spending their time fighting among themselves, also causing casualties among the pups. Today the Pribilof fur seal numbers nearly two million despite a crop of 50,000 or more skins being taken annually. The plan has been copied elsewhere in the world with similar beneficial results.

Culled, not slaughtered

One of the differences between old-time sealing and the present-day exploitation is that we used to speak of seals being slaughtered, whereas today we say they are being 'culled'. Even the use of this euphemism does not wholly appease public sentiment, which tends towards taking the side of the seals against the sealers. We know, from what happens in seal colonies elsewhere, for example on the Farne islands off the northeast coast of England, that protection can bring overcrowding and this in turn leads to disease and death, the natural way in which animal populations are kept down to a favourable level. Under these circumstances a controlled cull is ordered to reduce the swelling population to the proportions that will benefit the seals themselves. So controlled sealing not only preserves the species and enables a reasonable crop to be harvested but it also prevents overcrowding, which can do great harm to the animals themselves and it can be done in a virtually painless way.

International interest

Every year now there is a cull of seal pups in the Gulf of St Lawrence. It should be a private Canadian affair, but it has become one of international interest. This has developed into a spectacle in which sealers gather to club the pups for their pelts and seal sympathizers use any device they can think up to impede. The question is whether it is the culling of the seals *per se* that revolts them or evidence of actual cruelty in the killing. It is interesting, therefore, to turn to the results of a research done in 1967.

In that year Elizabeth Simpson of the School of Veterinary Medicine at

the University of Cambridge observed the culling of the Pribilof fur seal and similarly observed the harp seal hunt in the Gulf of St Lawrence. She was financed by the World Federation for the Protection of Animals with the assistance of the United States Bureau of Commercial Fisheries, Department of the Interior. She conducted *post mortem* examinations of 1121 seals out of 16,578 killed with hardwood clubs. After being clubbed the seal is laid out and an incision made in the chest with a knife aimed at the heart, to further ensure a speedy death. If the killing is not 'clean' the skull shows no fracture and only one point nine per cent of the 1121 skulls examined showed no fracture.

In the Gulf of St Lawrence only 154 skulls could be examined and of these thirty-six per cent were not fractured. On this basis it can be said impartially that there seems to be a higher possibility of needless cruelty in a St Lawrence cull as compared with cropping of Pribilof seals.

Elizabeth Simpson gave her own analysis of this. It was that on the Pribilofs the men clubbing the seals are experienced, work in small groups, under close supervision. They are supported by a team of workers to complete the operation. The seals are on land, where they can be readily rounded up into small groups. The sealers work for only four hours a day, have frequent breaks for refreshment and are salaried employees. In the Gulf of St Lawrence she found untrained sealers working over a large area of broken ice for twelve hours each day and paid by the piece. Each man both killed and skinned the harp seal pup. On the Pribilofs 60,000 seals are killed in six weeks. In the Gulf 50,000 are killed in three to five days. Simpson concludes 'as long as the present structure of exploitation of the harp seal in the Gulf of St Lawrence remains, humane killing does not seem likely'.

Left: a sealskin coat

Below left: an adult female Harp seal and her dead pup

Below: a seal hunter dragging a carcase away

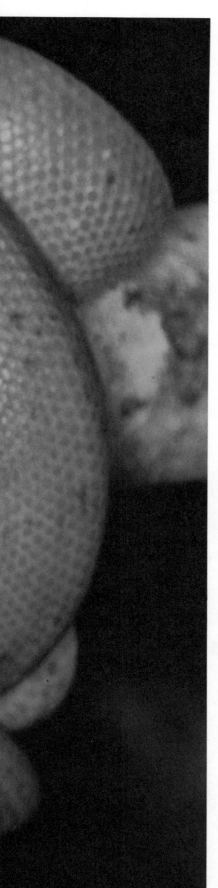

SAVING THE WORLD'S REPTILES

Snake   Turtle   Swamp turtle   Crocodile   Iguana
Galapagos tortoise   Angonoka tortoise

Throughout history reptiles have been shunned by man, and even today many are regarded if not with disgust, at least with a measure of distrust. It is certainly true that some species are a threat to man. Snakes will bite and crocodiles will attack in some areas, but man's tradition of dislike has come about mostly because the creatures tend to be somewhat unattractive. In general reptiles are less harmful than is supposed, and it has only recently been realized that many species are in jeopardy and in drastic need of protection.

Crocodiles have aroused little sympathy, but prejudices against them have been nothing like as harmful as the demand for hide for shoes, handbags and the like. Snakes have been victimized in a similar way. The giant Galapagos tortoises, once so numerous that the islands were named for them, were killed in great numbers for their oil and palatable flesh. Turtles have been exploited for centuries, their eggs have been eaten as well as their flesh, and the 'prehistoric' iguana has been a victim of tourism.

In addition to the more common crocodilians, snakes, tortoises and turtles, there are two less well known reptiles meriting mention.

The swamp turtle, of Western Australia, is one of the world's still-surviving primitives and the Angonoka tortoise, the world's rarest reptile, was in danger of becoming extinct until a breeding colony was started.

This section outlines ways in which the reptiles are being preserved, in some cases even simultaneously with supplying the skin trade.

The skin of a Cook's tree boa might vary in colour from green to red

Snake: *skins for luxury goods*

For most people snakes are to be shunned, avoided as much as possible. In many parts of the world, however, snake flesh has been and still is eaten as a delicacy or used as a medicine. Other parts of the body had their uses, as charms and other small-scale manufactures: the head for example, was used on musical instruments, for decoration. Even the skin has been used as leather, probably for as long as leathers in general have been used. Then, following the First World War, there was a world-wide shortage of leather. Only then were the possibilities of exploiting snake skin examined.

The 'big snakes'

Most snakes are too small for skinning them for leather to be worth while, but a python or a boa is a different proposition, owing to the great lengths they can attain: anaconda up to thirty-seven feet; reticulated python, thirty-three feet; African rock python, twenty-five feet; amethystine python, twenty-two feet; Indian python, twenty feet and the boa constrictor, nineteen feet. As well as the length, these non-venomous snakes have a fair girth, so any one of them will yield a fair-sized strip of leather for making shoe uppers, handbags, belts, chair covers, hats, together with coverings for cigarette cases, lighters, cameras, even for covering handles of tennis rackets.

Although smaller snakes were generally disregarded, the wart snakes of the Malay Archipelago were an exception. Also known as water snakes, the females may reach six feet in length and they are heavy-bodied, giving them a fair girth and therefore a fair width when the skin has been cured and laid flat. Their skin is granular, the scales do not overlap as in other

A common African python. With its length and girth it has a skin which would yield a fair-sized strip of leather

snakes and there are no ventral plates. It makes the best snake leather, especially for women's shoes and handbags.

Snakes periodically slough their skins and these can be seen occasionally lying around. A sloughed skin is of paper thickness, delicate and fragile, because it is only the surface layer. This surface layer is, in fact, removed anyway in preparing a skin for the market. The main skin is tough, made up of collagen fibres, with the tensile strength of steel wire. It needs to be since its owner must be able to crawl over all kinds of terrain, rough or smooth, dry or wet. There is no protection for it, so it needs to be highly durable.

The 'twenties boom

In world commerce there is no mention of snake leather before 1920. Then it suddenly appeared on the market backed by extensive advertising campaigns, which extolled snake leather as being easy to clean, durable, damp-proof and waterproof, and it was further recommended because it neither cracks, chips nor peels. It also has a pleasing pattern, so much so that it was thought worth while to make fake snake skins; cheaper leather ornamented with the pattern resembling that of real snake skin. Snake skin in the 1920s enjoyed a tremendous boom.

When we come to consider how much of a drain is being made on the world population of snakes there is difficulty in comparing the trade data. The classifications vary from country to country, some figures dealing in raw skins, others in tanned skins. Some trade returns are given by weight, others in numbers of skins handled. Much of the snake-skin products consist of imports into the United Kingdom, which acts as a clearing house for re-export to all parts of the world. The latest figures available are for 1976 and study of these allows a few generalizations to be made.

Whole snake skins on sale, as well as bags and purses made from smaller pieces. Crocodile-skin goods are also on display

The countries of origin are predominantly southern and southeastern Asia, particularly India, with Africa and South America decidedly secondary. The species represented are the Indian rat snake (107,109 skins) and the olivaceous keel-back snake (23,176 skins), from India, the reticulated python (1326 skins) and the elephant's trunk snake (22,875 skins), from southeastern Asia, the African rock python (2245 skins), the anaconda (ninety-six skins) and the boa constrictor (337 skins), from South America.

These figures may be regarded as minimal. For example, the returns for the African rock python read: 2245 skins plus 5877 metres, the second figure representing perhaps another thousand skins.

Disturbance of the environment

Although the losses to the wild snake fauna would appear to be considerable, it is impossible to say what percentage of the whole is taken annually for the skin trade, merely because no censuses have been made of the populations of the snakes as a whole. What we can say is that in Europe, which contains no snake of commercial value, there has been a marked decline in numbers in recent years, largely due to disturbance of the environment. The high probability is that there has been a similar decline for the Asian, African and South American species used in the trade, from this same cause, and that this may be more serious than the losses caused by collecting for the trade. There is no indication from other sources of any species of snake being endangered, except in heavily industrialized parts of Europe. Moreover, when we turn to the figures for the export of tanned skins from India there is a marked drop from 1970 onwards.

Above: the reticulated python of the Indo-Malaysian archipelago is by far the longest of the giant pythons, reaching a length of up to thirty-three feet

Right: an anaconda swimming in the Amazon river. Since this boa is a water snake it is difficult to judge the dimensions of the reptile and there have been reports of them reaching absurd lengths. This particular one would probably be about thirty feet, with a girth of at least two feet and weighing over half a ton

Turtle

Turtle: *wise use of a natural resource*

In a wide belt around the earth the tropical seas are spangled with islands large and, mainly, small—a sort of earthly milky way. Their sandy beaches, even on the smallest islands, as well as those on the shores of the continents, are potential nesting grounds for marine turtles. These rookeries, as they are called, are so numerous, widespread and often so inaccessible, except to the indigenous inhabitants, that no man living has ever made a complete list of them or has studied all of them.

We can, therefore, deal only in generalities. What we can say positively is that up to a hundred years ago the tropical seas must have been teeming with the seven species of living marine turtles, largely unseen because they spend much of their time just below the surface of the sea. The next generalization we can make, again with confidence, is that this vast biomass has declined catastrophically in the last few decades and that the drain on this natural resource, unchecked, could lead to the virtual extinction of some, if not all, of the seven species in the foreseeable future.

A further, fairly positive generalization that can be made is that the decline is being checked, mainly through the efforts of a relatively few dedicated men. These pioneers are all represented collectively by the IUCN Survival Commission Turtle Group and individually by Professor Archie Carr (named as the world's leading turtler), Dr Robert Bustard and Jack Frazier, to name but three. Assisting also is the World Wildlife Fund, especially the American National Appeal branch of it, and the Fauna Preservation Society of Great Britain.

For countless centuries the people living near the rookeries have exploited the turtles. They ate their eggs and they killed the adults for their

Above: a beach full of Pacific Ridley hatchlings making their way down to the sea

Left: a group of Pacific Ridley turtles depositing eggs

meat. They also made use of the shell, usually fashioning parts of it into objects for personal adornment and made leather from the skin. Theirs was an unlimited resource, as we can tell from a newly discovered rookery of the Pacific Ridley turtle in Orissa, northeastern India, found as recently as 1974. When first found, a count revealed 158,161 nesting turtles. So, in bygone times, these people were taking so small a proportion of the total as to make no difference.

A billion eggs a year

Female turtles do not lay every year as a rule, but every two to three years. Then, they lay up to eight times in a season at fortnightly intervals, each clutch containing sixty to ninety eggs. If we assume that on average each female lays three times in a season an average of seventy eggs each time, this means over thirty million eggs a season in this one rookery at Orissa. Jack Frazier, who for seven years studied the turtles of the Indian Ocean estimated that over an area of a million square miles hundreds of thousands of turtles nest annually. This is, to say the least, a conservative estimate, but using what has been called a guestimate we can imagine the total crop to be anything up to a billion eggs a year. This figure has, however, to be put in perspective. Of every thousand eggs laid only two or three hatchlings, at most, reach maturity.

The losses begin at nesting time. The females themselves are not always clever. Sometimes a late breeder will dig a pit for her eggs where a clutch has been previously laid, breaking or scattering the other eggs. In other cases the female, hauling ashore at low tide, lays her eggs below high tide mark and jackals are known to dig out nests. In one instance, on the Coromandel coast of southeastern India, in 1976, it is known that of forty nests thirty-four were destroyed by dogs and jackals. Then, when the hatchlings come to the surface and make their way to the sea the real carnage begins. They are prey of dogs and other carnivores, gulls, rats and crabs, and once in the water are attacked by fish. This is the vulnerable stage and any that survive it have only sharks—especially the tiger shark and the maneater—to contend with, as well as killer whales, and, of course, man. Many adult turtles have been found with one or more flippers bitten off by sharks, and grown turtles, whole or as remnants, have been taken from the stomachs of sharks.

Cash crop

All these, apart perhaps from the dogs, are no more than necessary checks on the total population, keeping it relatively stable. Even when people began taking the eggs and killing the adults the yearly losses would have been readily replaced because they represented only a small percentage of the total. It was when man began to see in the turtle harvest not only a means of subsistence but a cash crop that matters began to get out of hand, especially when the cash crop grew into a major item of commerce.

Catastrophic fall in numbers

The largest of the seven species is the leatherback, also known as the leathery turtle or luth. It may achieve a length of ten feet. The two species most used in commerce are the green turtle and the hawksbill, the first being used for soup and, later, filleted steaks, the second yielding the well-known tortoiseshell. Both became the basis of a flourishing export trade from tropical countries to the developing countries in Europe and, later, North America. Nevertheless, it seems agreed that even this did not cause the catastrophic fall in numbers that led to the alarm being sounded in the 1960s. Nor did this early commerce account for the declining populations in the other five species, including the leatherback. For that we have to go first to the root cause, the collecting and eating of turtle eggs on the spot, combined with the killing of grown turtles for their meat, together with dramatic increases in the human population. Thus, in 1971, it was reported that 'everyone in San Salvador eats turtle eggs'. The habit probably started when the population of San Salvador was a few thousand or tens of thousands. By 1971 it was around three million. Proportional increases can be assumed for other areas where there are nesting beaches.

Similarly, where the adults are also taken the increases in local human populations would have a proportionate devastating effect. These increases also mean expansion of activities some of which affect the

Right: leatherbacks, in Guyana, returning to the sea after laying their eggs

Below: the eggs are collected from the passive leatherback turtle as they are laid. Turtle eggs are considered a great delicacy and their popularity has done much to contribute to the serious drop in turtle numbers

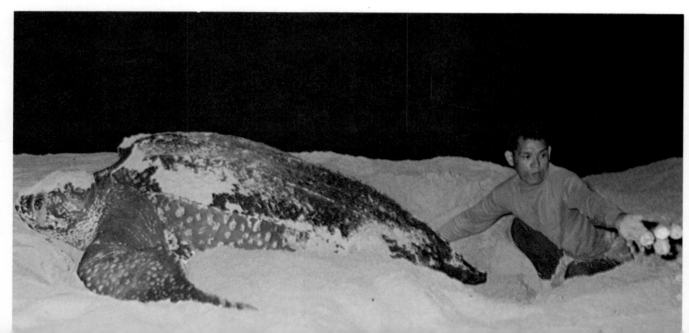

beaches directly or indirectly, so ruining the habitat of the turtles, especially the rookeries. And when, to these, are added the phenomenal increase in tourism, with the building of roads, hotels, local seaside amenities and the rest, the restriction of the habitat can be more easily imagined than described. On top of this there has been an increase in the export markets for turtle products, which can be illustrated by a few random statistics. Thus, in 1975 no turtles were protected in India and many coastal and inland towns in Orissa, Bengal, Kerala, the Andamans and Maldives had a thriving turtle industry based on the green turtle. The turtles were collected, their throats cut, the blood drunk, the meat, fat and guts all sold, each adult turtle yielding ninety to 100 pounds of meat, and the shell was cut into lengths and sold. At Turicorin alone 1500 turtles were killed annually.

Baby green turtles emerging from their leathery eggs. Although they weigh less than an ounce at birth, they eventually reach a weight of up to 300 pounds

Trade in tortoiseshell

In the same year, on Trinidad, 100 per cent of all females entering the rookeries were killed. For the years 1963-71 the catches in Hawaii increased fifty-fold. In 1976 the hawksbill was reported to be declining rapidly in both the Atlantic and Caribbean as a result of supplying tortoiseshell to Japan alone. Japan imported half a million pounds of tortoiseshell from Panama, Nicaragua, Cuba, the Cayman islands, as well as the Philippines, Indonesia, Singapore, Kenya and Tanzania. In 1972-3 a Japanese refrigerator ship collected large quantities of the East Pacific green turtle, known locally as the black turtle, from the Galapagos.

Not only is the trade in turtle products international, so are the movements of the turtles. The longest proved migration was by a leatherback tagged off Surinam and recovered off Ghana, a distance of 3700 miles in a direct line. Protective measures also need to be international, but only once was this nearly achieved. It is worth recalling it, however, because of the problems it underlines. In 1969 Costa Rica, Nicaragua and Panama reached agreement to protect the green turtle. This was important because the only known breeding ground in the Caribbean was on Costa Rica. Off Nicaragua were the beds of turtle grass on which the turtles fed and their resident or migratory grounds were off Panama. Protection from all three countries would have been the perfect arrangement. Nicaragua soon revoked the agreement and, to ruin things

Above: catching and immobilizing green turtles

Above right: the green turtle, once an important local food source

completely built two new processing plants. So the ideal plan collapsed.

Some countries have put a minimum size limit, below which it is illegal to kill turtles. This condemns the mature turtles, which unfortunately form the breeding population, whereas the smaller subadult turtles are expendable. For instance, Mexico prohibited the taking of eggs (although these continued to be offered for sale!), but did not put an embargo on the meat of Kemp's Atlantic Ridley turtle, which by 1977 became so scarce it was estimated it would become extinct within two years if nothing were done. The population had crashed from 160,000 in 1947 to 5000 or less in 1977. One cause was that in the shrimp-trawling that takes place off the coast of Mexico the turtles became enmeshed in the nets and were drowned. The World Wildlife Fund appealed for no shrimp-trawling in the area of Rancho Nuevo, north of Tampico, from April to July and for the twenty-mile beach to be declared a sanctuary extending twenty miles out to sea.

Government action

Many governments have taken action to protect their turtles with more or less willingness and effectiveness. Sometimes a close season is laid down, but not in all instances does this cover the breeding season, the time of greatest risk, when the gravid females are hauling out on to the beaches. Or again, legislation is enacted but not always enforced, or is allowed to be abortive, if not actually revoked, after pressure by trade interests. The United States and some other countries have sought a solution by prohibiting the import of all turtle products, but as already seen, Japan is still in the market and she is not alone. This is only part of the unevenness of turtle conservation.

Pressure of commercial interests

The Thai navy is reported to be helping to conserve its five species of turtles, which have decreased by eighty per cent in recent years. The Seychelles government has prohibited the export of caret shell — to conserve the hawksbill, so that the local craftsmen can continue to produce tortoiseshell objects and jewellery—but is under pressure by the commercial interests to relax its protection of the turtles. Some nations (including Sri Lanka, which gives full protection) have declared national parks or other forms of sanctuary around the breeding beaches.

Although the turtle has been a significant food resource for the people of the shores and islands of the Atlantic coast, the slaughter is not wholly attributable to the 'local' population

An obvious remedy, which would go a long way towards ironing out the inequalities, would seem to be turtle-farming and in 1970 a company known as Mariculture began such an venture in the Grand Caymans, taking eggs from the wild and rearing the hatchlings in tanks. In 1973 they had the first eggs, 4000 or more, laid in captivity. If this could have been maintained and extended the farm could have supplied the trade while leaving the wild populations intact. There was great promise in this, yet the venture failed largely, it is believed, because the United States and others had meanwhile enacted legislation banning imports of turtle products. The turtle farm is now American-owned. Another method of conserving the wild populations of turtles was tried in another part of the world. From 1961 to 1974 478,938 leatherback eggs were planted in hatcheries at Trengganu, Malaysia, and from these 244,392 hatchlings were released into the wild. It is estimated that about 2500 may reach maturity to be added to the wild population. A further 85,243 eggs were planted in 1975.

Protection while laying

Smaller efforts include one tried on Tobago by the Society for the Prevention of Cruelty to Animals, because the leatherbacks were consistently killed 'with revolting cruelty'. Fifty dollars were offered for each leatherback female protected while laying and escorted safely to the sea. In the first year this was tried there were, for the first time, no dead leatherbacks on the beaches—but the Society overspent its funds. Another method was tried in 1975, in the Seychelles, where the nests of the green turtle and the hawksbill had become much reduced. Marker buoys were placed half a mile from the shore, indicating a prohibited zone and the nesting sites on the rookeries were protected with wire netting.

No matter how well intentioned schemes may be there is usually the poacher to be reckoned with and the only scheme that seems to be a likely permanent success is that established in Queensland, Australia, by Robert Bustard. He persuaded the government to give protection to all turtles, including the hawksbill. With aid from IUCN and the American National Appeal of the World Wildlife Fund he set up experimental farms in Torres Straits, on the numerous islands between Australia and Papua-New Guinea. The islanders had long been taking the eggs and eating the turtles. Bustard showed that, by farming, turtles nine to twelve inches long could be produced in a year and that these could be exploited, for example by stuffing the shells and exporting them to be sold as curios to tourists. The islanders appreciated the commercial potential and instead of eating the eggs now raise the turtles and sell them.

Conservation is the rational exploitation of a natural resource, and rational exploitation means taking no more than the population can stand without decreasing in numbers. With wise husbandry on a global scale, by complete international agreement, the marine turtles could be restored to their former numbers and in time yield sufficient turtle products to satisfy what is obviously a huge world demand—if only the poacher could be converted and enlisted, as in Bustard's scheme.

A young green turtle being transported to market at Port Antonio, Jamaica. This is the easiest way of carrying such a load, which will almost certainly end its days in a stew pot

Swamp turtle: *a surviving primitive*

By contrast with the marine turtles, which not uncommonly make journeys of a thousand miles or more, the swamp or short-necked turtle, only six inches long, of Western Australia, is a stay-at-home. In common with other Australian freshwater turtles it can only withdraw its head into its shell for protection by bending its neck sideways and wedging its head between the upper shell, or carapace, and the abdominal shell, or plastron. It has another peculiarity. None of the 250 species of turtle and tortoise living today has advanced very far along the evolutionary trail from those living 120 million years ago and the swamp turtle has advanced less than most. The arrangement of the plates on the plastron of the swamp turtle shows affinities with those turtles living then, in the Cretaceous period. So the swamp turtle qualifies as the most primitive turtle still surviving.

The species was first identified from a specimen in the Vienna Museum that was sent there in 1839 by Dr L. Preiss, one of the most avid collectors of that century. All that was known of it was that it came from 'New Holland' and nothing more was known of it until 1907, when another specimen was found at Bullsbrook, twenty-five miles north of Perth, in

Two eight-day-old swamp turtles with an Australian coin, which has a diameter of twenty-six millimetres

what is called the crab-hole country. This consists of consolidated sand dunes on clay, where there are pools of water during the winter only, in which the turtle feeds mainly on tadpoles and other small aquatic animals. The area of swamp inhabited by the swamp turtles is now no more than 100 acres in extent, although it was much larger formerly, before the surrounding country was drained to give pastureland.

Appeal for money

The next swamp turtle turned up in 1954 and since then several more have been found and it is estimated that there may be between 200 and 300 still around. Conservationists set to work with an appeal for money to fence off 750 acres of what remains of the crab-hole country to preserve what is left of the turtle, for in spite of searches in similar terrain in the region the swamp turtle has not been located outside the Bullsbrook area.

Then, in 1967, plans were made to run an underground cable from Perth to Carnarvon. This would have gone straight through the Bullsbrook sanctuary, threatening the survival of this interesting living fossil, of which so little was known. Conservationists immediately went into action again. The mere presence of the cable would probably do little harm, but the work involved in laying it might do irreparable damage to the species. In the end, the cable was re-routed, at considerable additional cost.

Measuring the carapace of a swamp turtle. The nick in the shell was made by researchers as part of a numbering system

Crocodile: *saving the reptile and supplying the skin trade*

There are twenty-one species of crocodilians, called variously crocodiles, alligators, caimans and gharials, and the continued existence of at least fifteen of these is in peril. Crocodilians arouse little public sympathy and throughout the ages have been regarded more with distaste than anything else, largely for their attacks on human beings. Yet strangely, not all are a menace to life and limb. Even those with a record for man-killing may be dangerous in one area of their range, harmless in another.

Crocodilians are regarded as vermin where rivers are fished because of a supposed competition with fishermen and because they damage nets. Yet careful studies have shown that their presence is a benefit to the ecology of rivers and lakes, ensuring the populations of the fish they prey upon.

The long-standing prejudices against them, based mainly on ignorance and superstition, were nothing like as damaging to their survival as the effects of a sudden demand for crocodile hide, for shoes, handbags and the like, during the last few decades. Such was the demand and the consequent carnage that in some places whole areas were swept clean of them. First, all the large crocodiles were shot out and even small ones were not safe. Statistics from Uganda illustrate this. At first the crocodiles killed were seven feet or more long. In 1965 they averaged three and a half feet, in 1968 two and a half feet.

Drain on crocodilians

A few years ago a newspaper report told of a crocodile hunter, receiving news that someone had seen a small crocodile, actually hired a plane to go and shoot it for its skin. The story may have been exaggerated, even apocryphal, but it epitomized what was happening. At the same time there came a lesser, but still considerable, drain on the world's crocodilians when a widespread craze for keeping the small ones as pets developed. A smaller but contributory cause was the stuffing of dried skins of baby crocodiles and setting them in grotesque attitudes for sale as curios or souvenirs to tourists. The use of power-driven launches on large lakes, creating waves, also disturbs the crocodiles and damages the nests.

As always the high prices paid for skins led to over-hunting, so the traders enlisted the help of local peoples, supplying them with torches—and salt for curing the skins—to look for crocodiles in inaccessible places at night, shining the light into their eyes. Governments placed embargoes on the trade in skins and passed legislation protecting the reptiles, but as usual the traders did not want to know and the local poachers cared even less about the restrictions.

Eating the seed corn

The problem of the disappearing crocodilians was world-wide; in all warm areas of the globe. And it was the same story everywhere. One of the most damaging aspects is that crocodilians, whether crocodile, alligator, caiman or gharial, do not start to breed until they are large. The Nile crocodile, for example, the common crocodile of Africa, and the one hardest hit by the skin trade, is a foot long at birth, grows ten inches a year and breeds when nine to eleven feet long. The largest ever measured was sixteen feet long. The most valuable skins are obtained from medium-sized crocodiles, six to ten feet long. So the killing of medium to large sizes means eating the seed corn. In this case, killing the animals before they have had a chance to breed. Moreover, as the medium to large sizes are used up hunters turn to ever smaller animals to satisfy trade demands.

In the opinion of H. Robert Bustard, who has made a greater study of

Nile crocodiles. One of the largest of the crocodilians, reaching approximately sixteen feet and weighing 2000 pounds. It once ranged from the Cape of Good Hope, across much of Africa and down the Nile valley into the Mediterranean, but today is restricted to isolated preserves

the threat to the world's crocodilians than anyone else, the best hope for conserving the crocodilians everywhere is to build up the numbers to enable the industry to thrive on a sustained yield basis. Only then will people accept crocodile conservation as sensible, practicable and profitable. In the light of these pronouncements we turn to what is happening at the Spencer's Creek Crocodile Ranch on the banks of the Zambezi river, near the famous Victoria Falls in Rhodesia, and at other farms elsewhere.

Problems of farming

Ideally, a ranch should include breeding adults, but the objections to this are great. Firstly, it is impossible to tell male from female without cutting open the body. Secondly, the high cost of feeding them would make the venture uneconomical. Thirdly, much space would be needed not only for the normal housing of large numbers of big crocodiles, but in addition, large areas would be needed for the nests, which are usually well spaced out. Nevertheless, successful crocodile-farming seems to have been achieved in Thailand by keeping breeding adults in captivity.

The problem is solved in Rhodesia by collecting the eggs from the wild; and the ranch is licensed to take 2500 eggs a year, found by following the tracks in the mud made by the female going to the nesting site. This number of eggs, left in the wild, would produce at most twenty-five

Far left: an American alligator, seen here at the Everglades, Florida

Below: rough treatment and outright cruelty have often been the fate of crocodilians

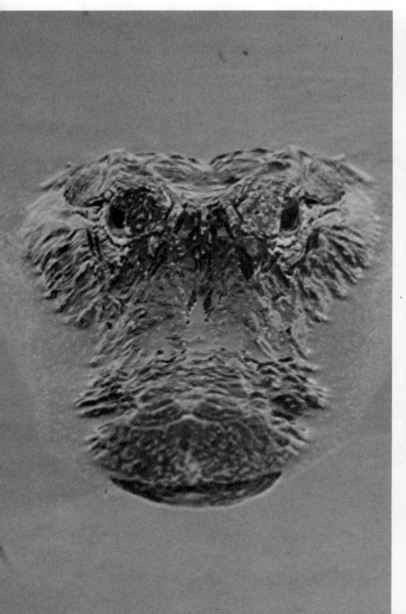

medium-sized crocodiles in five to ten years. The rest would be eaten as eggs by the Nile monitor, a lizard, among others, or as young by fish eagles, marabou storks and larger crocodiles. This wastage is avoided on a ranch. Another killer of baby crocodiles is disease, especially gastroenteritis and pneumonia. Disease is kept low on the ranch by feeding the babies on minced offal fortified with vitamins.

Success in captivity

The eggs are kept in boxes at constant temperatures around ninety degrees Fahrenheit and constant humidity. On hatching the babies are transferred to shallow ponds and carefully watched. Each age group is thereafter kept in a separate walled-in enclosure containing a concrete-lined pool fifty feet long by six feet wide and over two feet deep. Every twenty-four hours the ponds are emptied, scrubbed and refilled with fresh water from the Zambezi river. One result of the hygienic conditions and regular feeding is that the crocodiles grow twice as fast as in the wild. The survival rate from the egg stage is seventy per cent, whereas in the wild it would be five per cent or less. Natural losses in the wild are increased by interference from development, such as the building of hydroelectric dams. Logging mahogany in Belize caused a severe drop in the numbers of crocodiles. The increase in tourism, with the building of hotels and bigger motorboats being used for pleasure, creating larger and larger waves

Once common in the estuaries and river courses of the coastal regions from North Carolina to Texas, the range of the American alligator is now severely reduced and it is protected everywhere

which inundate the banks, bears directly on the problem. Unfortunately tourism is often heaviest in the breeding and nesting season. In addition crocodile eggs are susceptible to damp and suffer in periods of unusually heavy rainfall.

One condition on which the licence is granted is that five per cent of three-year-olds must be returned to the wild in selected places. Currently there are five thousand crocodiles in the ranch, which means over a period of three years or so more than 200 crocodiles will be released at an age when they are past the vulnerable stage.

Ranching economies

At the age of three years the remaining ninety-five per cent of crocodiles are shot through the ear, death being instantaneous. The skin is unharmed for commercial purposes and the killing is economical in another sense. Crocodiles swallow pebbles (for use as ballast, it is always said) and it is not uncommon for a crocodile shot in a river to sink and be totally lost, carried down by its own ballast. A further economy on a ranch is that nothing of the carcase is wasted. The flesh is used to feed the other crocodiles—they are notorious cannibals, and in a natural state crocodiles sort themselves

Above left: a recently shot Nile crocodile is skinned to supply a ready demand for hide, to be used to make luxury goods such as bags, shoes and wallets. Only the under-belly is actually used

Above: a gruesome key ring made from the head of a young crocodile

Right: an Amazon caiman

out by age, so lessening the chances of the larger ones eating the smaller.

If a ready supply of skins could be ensured this would go a long way towards satisfying the trade, but the five per cent released into the wild would still need to be placed in reserves. To release them anywhere else would be a waste of time because of poaching.

Total protection

In the United States desirable results were achieved in 1966 by another method, by giving alligators total protection. This did not eliminate poaching and for the years 1968 to 1970 127,000 skins were taken illegally, according to the records of one dealer in Georgia alone. Forty poachers were taken to court, but it was believed that this number only represented one in every eleven poachers operating. Sales of crocodile or alligator products were made illegal in New York so the trade in poached skins was switched to Japan, where the skins were made into shoes, purses, jewellery and bags and cases of various kinds.

Even so, by 1973 in Florida there had been a fifty-per-cent increase in numbers and wildlife officials had had to deal with nearly 5000 complaints about alligators being a nuisance. Most of the offending crocodilians were translocated and a few 'rogues' had to be destroyed. In the same year, in an experimental alligator harvest programme in Louisiana, sixty-one hunters killed 1350 alligators averaging seven feet in length in a thirteen-day open

season. The Wildlife and Fisheries Commission reported that the cull seemed not to have affected the alligator population as a whole, that there was no evidence of skins being taken illegally. In June 1973, however, one of the Commission's special agents was found in possession of nearly a hundred freshly salted skins!

In 1977 it was reported that there were 600,000 alligators, representing three-quarters of America's alligators, in Florida and the coastal areas of Georgia, Louisiana, South Carolina and Texas, and for these places the alligator was removed from the Fish and Wildlife Services endangered species list. The name was, however, retained on the list for Alabama, Mississippi, Oklahoma and North Carolina and the interior of Georgia, Louisiana, South Carolina and Texas.

Governments, through their laws and wildlife services the world over are tackling the problem of the disappearing crocodilians, among the oldest of the world's inhabitants still surviving. By the sustained yield harvest, as shown by the Louisiana experiment, as well as by the setting up of ranches, the desirable twin objectives seem likely to be achieved of saving the crocodiles and supplying a likely increase in trade in skins.

Crocodilians are frequently vicious with each other and are notorious cannibals. These two fighting American alligators were seen on the Aranas National Wildlife Refuge, Texas

Iguana: *tourism instead of dodoism*

The large flightless pigeon known as the dodo lived on the island of Mauritius in the Indian Ocean. It became extinct in 1681. One of the few to be brought to Europe alive found itself in London, where it was exhibited in a shop window and, so the record goes, was fed on pebbles because that was what it was said to eat. 'Dodo' is from a Portuguese word meaning a simpleton. If the story from seventeenth-century London is to be believed, the name could have been applied equally appropriately to the people into whose hands it fell. The cause of the extinction of the species was that the Europeans who first settled on Mauritius took their pigs with them, and these ate both the eggs and the chicks of the dodo so that as the adults died there was no rising generation to take their places.

In the history of the dodo, as in a nutshell, is contained some of the commonest causes which the modern movement for conservation of wildlife seeks to counter: ignorance, the inhumanity that often springs from it and the devastating effects of killing off the younger generations, as

A Brazilian iguana. Of its total of seven feet length, a large proportion is taken up by the tail, which it uses as a defence system, by lashing out with it. Its visual powers are better than its sense of smell

Quite apart from its suffering at the hand of man, the Galapagos iguana has fallen victim to domestic animals gone feral. This iguana was killed by dogs

well as the damage resulting from domesticated animals that get out of hand. The present-day story of the world's iguanas contains all these elements and further lessons in addition.

The name 'iguana' is from a Caribbean word, *iwana*, for the local lizards that look something like the large prehistoric reptiles that died out eighty to a hundred million years ago. The resemblance is not as strong as some writers suggest, but there is a relationship. Iguanodons, the best known of the large extinct reptiles, have teeth similar to those of the living iguanas.

One of the more remarkable features of iguanas is their geographical distribution. Most of the species are concentrated in the Americas, but a few live in Fiji and Tonga in the South Pacific, and others are found in Malagasy. It is a distribution hard to explain.

No sympathy

Most people, even animal-lovers, have little sympathy for the reptiles, partly perhaps because they are cold-blooded and creep about, although iguanas can, when circumstances demand, show surprising agility and a fair turn of speed. This lack of sympathy, as well as the inhumanity shown them, is illustrated by the story brought back in 1974 by Christian Zuber from the island of Guadeloupe in the Caribbean. When he and his wife visited the small island of Saintes, near Guadeloupe, in 1971, the best place, they were told, to see iguanas, they counted two hundred of them, up to three feet long. In 1973 they visited the same area and saw between twenty-five and thirty-five only. Also, those remaining were markedly more shy than formerly.

They noticed that stuffed iguanas were on sale in shops for tourists in 1971, but they were told there were not many tourists. By the time of their second visit, day visits by charter flight from Miami and New York had been established and there were 'plenty tourists'. The local peoples were catching the iguanas, keeping them alive without water in large cans and killing and stuffing them when tourists were due. They usually killed them by opening them with a razor blade while still alive, because the backbone then came out more easily.

While dining with the governor of Guadeloupe, Zuber suggested that if they wished to cash in on a local product, the people of Saintes should build wooden hides, put out food to attract the iguanas and establish an even more profitable tourist attraction—tourism instead of dodoism.

A few years before this, attention had been drawn to the declining numbers of iguanas on the Galapagos islands. Apparently, in the days of the buccaneers, the tails of iguanas were a favoured delicacy, but the real damage was caused by goats taken to the islands by these same buccaneers. These ate the vegetation in which the young iguanas sheltered, so exposing them and making them an easy prey to the Galapagos hawk. Also, dogs and cats later taken to the islands had gone feral. The dogs killed iguanas of all sizes; the cats killed the young ones and ate them. The alarm was raised in 1977 and plans were made to bring survivors, especially from the islands of Santa Cruz and Isabela, to the Charles Darwin Research Station, there to breed them in captivity. At the same time a campaign to exterminate the feral dogs and cats was mounted.

Cruelty through ignorance

Nicaragua is another place where iguanas are taken for food. They have been described as a valuable natural resource. Their numbers are currently declining steeply because no effort is being made to control the hunters who catch them and sell them alive in markets. This increased trade in Nicaragua in live animals often involves cruelty due to ignorance.

Marine iguanas on Fernandina, Galapagos. It is thought that the species came by sea from South America, where iguanas are common, and colonized the Galapagos

In Fiji there is also concern at the falling numbers of the local iguana (*Brachylopus fasciatus*), which is one of the most distinctive of land animals. It is up to two feet long, the female bright green, the male banded green and brown. It is said to be rare throughout its range on the group of Fijian islands and although listed today as a threatened species, as recently as 1915 it was everywhere on the islands 'not uncommon'. It is not only now considered rare, but actually extinct on some of the islands.

Prejudice

The first disadvantage it suffers from is that Fijians kill it on sight, although whether from ignorance or superstition or merely from some irrational prejudice is not clear. There are two further causes for its decline. The first is that the introduced mongoose eats its eggs and young. The second is also linked with an introduced animal, the large rhinoceros beetle, which damages the coconut palms that are important to the island's economy. To control the ravages of the rhinoceros beetles the Fijians climb the coconut palms to kill them. In doing so they invade the natural retreat of the iguana into the crowns of the palms and, having a traditional prejudice against them, kill the iguanas whenever they see them among the palm fronds. There is an irony in this since the iguana normally feeds on beetles and other insects and, unmolested, would no doubt help considerably in eradicating the rhinoceros beetle.

There is another side to the iguana saga that is not without its

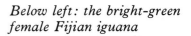

Below left: the bright-green female Fijian iguana

Below: Iguana tuberculata, *another striking green species*

importance in the general story of conservation. Michael Carey has studied two species of iguana in the Exuma Cays, a ninety-mile chain of islands in the Bahamas. The two species are Allan's Cays rock iguana (*Cyclura inornata*) and a closely related species (*Cyclura figginsi*). He had heard that one, possibly both, were extinct, exterminated largely by local fishermen and sportsmen. When he first landed on the island of Allan's Cays he at once saw two large individuals of the rock iguana foraging among the litter on the beach. Another was basking on an outcrop of rock near by. Altogether he found eighty to ninety on the island, which is only ten acres in extent, giving a density of eight two- to three-foot iguanas to the acre. This could be more suitably described as an island carrying its maximum load of iguanas.

Extinct or extant

Carey then points out that Allan's Cays rock iguana, and to a lesser extent the other species, have been alternately reported as extinct and extant, which was why he decided to investigate them. Even species that are normally numerous suffer fluctuations in numbers. A species may be unusually numerous for several years and then noticeably decreasing for several years, the rises and falls in the populations balancing out in the long run. When the numbers of a species are at a low ebb, such fluctuations could lead to contradictory reports over a period of years, varying from totally extinct to extant.

A marine Galapagos iguana. There are several local subspecies, which have varying amounts of brick-red blotching on the side of the body

Galapagos tortoise: *gentle giant*

The fossil record shows that hundreds of species of tortoises inhabited the world until relatively recent geological times. The largest among them had a shell eight feet long. Many of these species, including the largest, failed to survive on the mainland, but on the islands their size and the absence of large predators allowed some of the giant tortoises to continue until today, notably on the Galapagos, in the Pacific, off the coast of Ecuador, and on the Seychelles, in the Indian Ocean.

The Galapagos islands were discovered in 1535 by the Spanish explorer, Fray Tomas de Berlanga. The giant tortoises were so numerous then that the islands were named for them (*galapagos* being Spanish for tortoises). Their flesh proved to be palatable and the islands became a regular port of call for ships plying that part of the Pacific, where fresh water could be had as well as meat.

Nevertheless, William Dampier, the English navigator, was able to write in 1697 that 'the land turtles are so numerous that 500 or 600 men might subsist on them alone for several months, without any other sort of provision. They are extraordinarily large and fat, and so sweet that no

Aldabra giant tortoises half submerged in the cool of a freshwater pool

Abingdon's giant tortoise. This is supposedly the last specimen of this race

pullet eats more pleasantly'.

A certain Captain Porter of the United States frigate *Essex*, writing in 1812, told of calling at the Galapagos and in four days taking on board fourteen tons of tortoises. A mature tortoise may have a shell four feet long and its total weight may be up to 560 pounds. Given that not all the tortoises were that size, the ship was loaded with upwards of 700 tortoises, and all but three were females, because they are larger than the males. They were piled on the quarterdeck under an awning for a few days, to allow them to empty their bowels. Then they were stored below in the certain knowledge that, provided their shells were not broken, they would remain alive and healthy for a year without food or water—which is surprising since these large tortoises love to wallow and at the same time drink copiously. Presumably the atmosphere in the hold was cool and damp enough for them to survive.

Tortoises for oil

When Charles Darwin in 1838 visited the Galapagos, of which there are thirteen main islands, the giant tortoises were still numerous, but it had already been discovered that their fat could yield a clear oil, about three gallons from a fully grown tortoise. American whalers developed the habit of calling at the islands and loading up with tortoises, 300 at a time. With 700 whalers operating, taking some 200,000 a year from 1831 to 1867, it has been estimated that ten million tortoises were removed. Even if that figure is an over-estimate, the numbers must have run into hundreds of thousands.

By the end of that time the giant tortoises had been wiped out on several of the islands and were becoming rare on most of the others. It was no longer worth taking them for oil or for their meat. Left to themselves the tortoises would have recovered their numbers, to some extent at least, but for a fresh hazard. Man had inadvertently introduced the common rat. He had also taken ashore goats, pigs, cats and dogs, some of which had gone wild. Only the mature adult tortoises were safe from these.

In 1942 came a further menace, a series of droughts that converted the normally wet season of January to April to a dry season, year after year for the next twenty years, with the exception of 1953. The springs, waterfalls and pools dried up. Meanwhile the onslaught from feral animals continued. Pigs rooted out the eggs and ate them and also ate the young ones. Feral cats and dogs ate the young. Goats aided by donkeys and cattle devastated the vegetation on which the tortoises fed. Left to itself the situation would have ended in one way only: the complete extinction of the Galapagos giant tortoises, with a separate subspecies on each of the major islands that had meant so much to Charles Darwin in the formulation of his theory of the origin of species, during his voyage on the *Beagle*.

That anything positive was done to retrieve the situation is mainly to the credit of the dedicated Belgian conservationist Dr Victor van Straelen. Already, in 1959, he had persuaded the Ecuador government to declare all uninhabited parts of the islands a national park and to give full protection to, especially, the giant tortoise. In 1960 work was begun on the Charles Darwin Research Station on the Galapagos islands. Four years later the station was dedicated, the Galapagos International Scientific Project was instituted and an agreement was signed between the Charles Darwin Foundation and the government of Ecuador. This gave the Foundation special rights, privileges and responsibilities and the authority, from the Ecuador government, to take almost any steps it deemed right to safeguard the unique flora and fauna of the islands.

Offending ferals

The first step, simultaneous with making a scientific survey of the islands, was to liquidate the goats, dogs, pigs and other offending ferals, as well as the common rat, the latter being the most difficult task. In June of 1964 250 goats were shot, in July another 300. That this was only a beginning may be judged from the figures for the small island of Pinta, where in 1958 goats were first released. A male and two females were put ashore from a fishing boat to provide fresh meat for the fisherman's future visits. Ten years later, a team from the Darwin Research Station estimated that there were between 4000 and 5000 goats on the island, with a corresponding devastation of the vegetation.

In late 1964 a report was published about the state of the tortoises on the various islands. The largest surviving population was on Santa Cruz (Indefatigable island) and there was an abundant population in parts of Isabela (Albemarle). Pinzon (Duncan) island had some 140, all adult, the rats having consistently eaten the eggs and young. On Santiago (James) island the tortoises appeared to be extinct. None was found on Santa Fé (Barrington), Jarvis island and Pinta (Abingdon) island. Española (Hood) island yielded only three after a nine-day search; this was one of the islands visited by the whalers. It was also an island where poaching still went on and where there were many goats. On Chatham and Charles islands, together known as Floreana, the tortoises were extinct except for a very few on Chatham. Fernandina (Narborough) island has no tortoises: the assumption being that they were wiped out by volcanic activity.

Breeding in captivity

In 1971, twenty eggs of the Hood tortoise hatched at the Darwin Research Station. These were from three females and one male taken from seven seen since 1964. The hatchlings were destined to be returned to their native island. By 1972, seven of the eleven surviving subspecies were being successfully bred at the Station and, while hunting down the feral goats on Pinta, National Park Service guards found one endemic tortoise and tracks of two or three others where tortoises were thought to be extinct in 1964. In 1974 it was reported that on Española thirteen more had been found, giving a total of sixteen for the island, of which two only were males. Twelve of these were taken for breeding and produced forty-two young.

Giant tortoises in a mud-hole. The typical domed shell indicates a vegetarian. The tortoises comprise many different subspecies, which all arose from ancestors reaching the Galapagos islands from Ecuador

The Seychelles, named after King Louis XV (Moreau de Séchelles) of France, are a group of islands in the Indian Ocean to the north of Malagasy, the other side of the world from the Galapagos. They were first discovered by the Portuguese in about 1500 and remained uninhabited, except for pirates who used them as bases, until the French colonized them in 1744. Other islands in this region are Réunion, Mauritius and Rodriguez, as well as the island of Aldabra. There is reason to believe that in the sixteenth and seventeenth centuries giant tortoises existed on all islands of these groups, too. An idea of their numbers can be gained from the words of the French traveller and naturalist, François Leguat, who visited Rodriguez in 1961: '. . . there are such plenty of land-turtles in this isle that sometimes you see three thousand of them in a flock, so that you may go above a hundred paces on their backs'.

It is claimed that every island had its own species of giant tortoise, but they have been so translocated from one island to another, and have been so hybridized that today they are all classified as *Geochelone gigantea*.

Giant tortoises were still abundant in Mauritius in 1740, but by 1761 they were being imported from Rodriguez to feed patients in the hospitals. Ships are known to have brought 400 at a time. We have to assume that the giant tortoises on Mauritius had been exterminated; and before long the Rodriguez tortoise was extinct also. The giant tortoise on Réunion had vanished some time before that. The history of their disappearance from these islands is poorly documented. It is, however, known that in eleven months of 1759-60 over 30,000 giant tortoises were removed from Rodriguez alone. The one island that did not share this fate was Aldabra, and when the folly of total extermination was realized, and indiscriminate slaughter forbidden, Aldabra tortoises were shipped to other islands to re-stock them. Some were taken to the Seychelles, including the one that was later taken to Mauritius and became known as Marion's tortoise, from which we have the only indubitably authentic record of longevity, which is 152 years plus. Today giant tortoises, imported, are kept in a state of semi-domestication on the Seychelles.

Top: a Santa Cruz tortoise eating opuntia pads

Above: a giant tortoise eating grass. The long neck is possibly an adaptation which allowing browsing on cacti and low plants.

Complete eradication

Only two questions remain to be discussed. One is why giant tortoises should have been so completely eradicated on so many of the Indian Ocean islands. From such evidence as can be mustered it seems the answer must be that they were slaughtered, either on land or by ship's crews, who took them for a supply of fresh meat on long voyages, in an incredibly uncontrolled manner. The reptile's demise was probably hastened, as was that of the Galapagos tortoises, by the introduction of dogs, cats, rats and pigs that between them ate the eggs and young, and goats that devastated the vegetation on which the tortoises fed.

The other question remaining concerns the numbers left still on Aldabra. During the last sixty years a variety of estimates have been made. These range from complete extinction to few or numerous. In 1964-5 the Bristol Seychelles Expedition spent two periods of one month each on Aldabra and estimated there were 33,000 giant tortoises remaining. The most recent estimate is by David Bourn of Oxford University, who carried out what he describes as an extensive tortoise census and marking programme in 1973 and 1974. His estimate was of 150,000 giant tortoises on Aldabra, including, we may suppose, all the little ones.

Angonoka tortoise: *the world's rarest reptile*

In 1885, the noted French zoologist, L. Vaillant, came across a preserved specimen of a tortoise in the collections of the Frankfurt Museum. It bore no name and the label on it said merely 'near Aldabra' (Aldabra is an island in the Indian Ocean). Vaillant gave the tortoise the scientific name *Testudo yniphora* (now changed to *Geochelone yniphora*). In this way was introduced to the world at large what has been described as its rarest reptile, known by its vernacular name of angonoka.

Unusual feature

The shell of the angonoka is strikingly like that of the radiated tortoise of Malagasy, with similar radiating yellow or orange lines, but its most unusual feature is its gular (throat) plate, which projects well forward from the plastron (underpart of the shell) and curves upwards in such a way as to suggest that the animal may have difficulty in feeding effectively. The shell is up to eighteen inches long and the total weight is up to fifteen pounds.

It was later found that the angonoka is also native to Malagasy and the last published reference to it was in 1950 when it was predicted that the species would become extinct 'within only a few years'. In 1973 Dr Charles P. Blanc of the Université Paul Valéry in Montpellier, France, gave it as his opinion that only ten were surviving in the wild, all in the Soalala-Baly Bay area of northwestern Malagasy, with an unknown number in captivity in zoos in various different parts of the world, including Malagasy.

Rooted superstition

Blanc's assessment was based on an on-the-spot investigation made when, in 1971, he visited the Baly Bay area with James O. Juvik, Assistant Professor of Geography at the University of Hawaii. Apart from tracking the tortoises in their wild habitat, their inquiries showed some of the causes for the species being on the brink of extinction.

The first cause was the burning of the scrub and grassland to make the land available for agriculture. The second was the attitude of the local people. To them the tortoise was taboo as an article of diet, but they had a rooted superstition that the angonoka, merely by its presence, prevented disease in their chickens. Consequently, they had the custom, in some areas at least, of drilling a hole in the rear margin of the shell, to tether the tortoise near their huts.

Great delicacy

The main cause of threat, however, seems to have been the export of the tortoise in large numbers to the neighbouring island of Réunion, where the French residents treated it as a great delicacy. Juvik and Blanc also postulated that the species may be at the end of an evolutionary line due to over-specialization, and they pointed to the unusual gular plate, which they hypothesized, might restrict its feeding. This seems unlikely, however, since a similar elongation of the gular plate occurs also in the South African bowsprit tortoise, which seems not to have found it an obstacle to survival.

In fact, the Angonoka tortoise is almost certainly less handicapped in its feeding than plenty of birds that suffer injury to the beak or a pathological distortion of the beak. Such birds are not uncommon and they seem to adapt successfully to their disabilities.

After some hesitation, the two investigators decided to remove six of the tortoises they found and take them to Honolulu to try establishing a breeding colony there.

DECLINE OF THE OCEAN HARVEST

Sea mammals   Bluefin tuna   Krill   Porpoise
Sea monster   Fish

To many people the world's oceans and seas may seem to offer an unlimited supply of food resources and at the same time serve as a convenient dumping ground for whatever waste needs to be disposed of. But the reality is very different.

Methods of fishing have become so efficient and mechanized that what were once taken for granted as plentiful supplies of food fish are now to be a sadly dwindling resource. Fish are being caught smaller and smaller and the concept of 'eating the seed corn' is now a common phenomenon.

The world's marine harvest, particularly cod, herring, pollock and tuna are discussed in relation to the problems of overfishing, and the continuing battle over international fishing limits.

The whale has caused more concern than any other group of animals, and there has been much public action in support of 'saving the whale' and protecting all the various species from over-exploitation.

In the continual search for new fishing grounds to satisfy the ever-increasing world demand for food, it has been realized that the ocean is swarming with other forms of marine life which could be made use of. Krill, a two-inch crustacean is one such potential food source.

In the harvesting of the seas for food dishes there are occasionally accidental victims. Porpoises, which associate with tuna, get caught in the nets set for the fish, and, unable to surface to breath, are unfortunately drowned.

Finally, the oceans are still considered to be places of mystery and occasionally unidentified 'monsters' are dredged up, included in this section is an explanation of one such find.

The southern right whale after breaching

Sea mammals: *a delicate balance*

It would be fair to say that the fate of the whales and seals has evoked more public concern than that of any other group of animals. At its highest level, this concern has resulted in dedicated groups hiring boats to disrupt the hunting of whales, and seal hunters have had their boats burned and their lives threatened. Whether this is taking a concern for animal conservation too far is a matter of opinion, but there can be no doubt about the serious state of some whale and seal stocks. The posters exhort us to 'Save the Whale', but it does not come amiss to remember that there is more than one kind of whale and they have many problems facing them. The same holds true for seals. Some populations of seals are on the brink of extinction while others are burgeoning.

Depleted stocks

By the late 1960s stocks of the great whales were becoming seriously depleted. Blue, humpback, gray whales and the right whales were protected, but protection only came after each species was nearing extinction. Similarly, quotas set for other species—sperm, fin, sei and minke—were progressively reduced only when numbers had already begun to diminish. A major change in the regulation of whaling came in 1972 at the meeting of the International Whaling Commission (IWC). The system of Blue Whale Units (BWU) was dropped in favour of separate quotas for each species. In the BWU system whaling fleets were allotted a number of BWUs (one BWU = one blue whale, two fin whales, two and a half humpbacks or six sei whales). Within this limit they could catch species in any proportion.

Quotas set for the 1978 season		
NORTH ATLANTIC		
Sperm		685
Minke		2555
Fin		459
Sei		84
NORTH PACIFIC		
Sperm		
male	5105	
female	1339	6444
Bryde's		524
Minke		400
SOUTHERN HEMISPHERE		
Sperm		
male	4538	
female	1370	5908
Minke		5690
Sei		771
		23,520

Also in 1972, the UN Conference on the Human Environment called for a ten-year ban on whaling, but the IWC felt that the new quota system was sufficient to protect the whales from over-exploitation. Whale conservationists maintain that quotas have been set too high for the safety of the species and that they fail to take into account two things. Not enough is known of the biology of some species—their rate of reproduction for instance—nor of the size of the populations. Secondly, whales are social animals and the killing of one or more members of a group could seriously disrupt its social organization and affect breeding. (See table for the quotas that were set for the 1978 season.)

Loopholes

In theory the IWC is doing its work well, but, apart from fears that quotas are too large, there are loopholes in the system. Not every nation engaged in whaling is a member of the Commission, and they do not have to comply with its regulations. Even member nations can withdraw their support and a new development is Japan (a member nation) teaming up with non-member nations to beat the quotas.

There still remains the problem of whether it is justifiable to hunt these intelligent animals. Research is being made into finding more humane methods of killing whales, but is there a compelling reason for continuing the hunt? The United States Government has gone so far as to ban the import of all whale products. Whale oil can be largely substituted by vegetable oils, but the Japanese in particular use the meat for human consumption. Sperm whale oil has long been used essentially for lubricating delicate machinery, but a substitute has been found in meadow foam and jojoba, two plants that grow in the dry, southwestern states.

The trend in modern whaling has been to hunt the largest whales. There

Below left: curiosity on both sides. A southern right whale showing as much interest in man as vice versa

Below: primitive methods of hunting whales are still being used in a few places. This sperm whale is being harpooned from a rowing boat; a risky business since small craft can easily be overturned by an angry whale

is no point in chasing a comparative pygmy like a minke whale when there are blue whales about. This resulted in near-destruction of the blue whale. Then the whalers turned their attentions to the second-largest whale, the fin whale. When this species became scarce, it was the turn of the sei whale, and so on. Within the last decade, the scarcity of great whales has forced whalers to turn to medium whales—killer, bottlenose, pilot and beaked whales—which previously they would never have considered worth pursuing. North Atlantic bottlenose whales are now protected by the IWC.

Accidental deaths

The small whales—porpoises—have no protection and are hunted in many places, but the most recent threat has come in the eastern Pacific, where two species, the spotted porpoise and the spinner porpoise, have been killed in colossal numbers. In 1971 it was estimated that 184,000 spotted porpoises and 129,000 spinner porpoises were killed. All these deaths were accidental! The porpoises were trapped and drowned in purse seine nets set for yellowfin tuna. Schools of porpoises associate with shoals of tuna, so showing the fishermen where to set their nets. Since 1971 attempts have been made to find ways of letting the porpoises escape from the nets and the numbers killed have dropped, but both species are declining.

Above: fin whales at a whaling station in the Antarctic. Whales are attracted to the area because of the concentration of krill. Once hunted on a massive scale, today only limited numbers are caught

Above right: a whale breaching. This magnificent spectacle can be an expression of either joy or anger. The whale is a mammal of immense strength and this movement is achieved by a flicking action of the tail

The question now is whether protection has come in time for some whales. The blue whale appears to be recovering very slowly with a population in the Antarctic of around 10,000. Californian gray whales now have a stable population of about 11,000, not far below the pre-whaling estimate of 15,000. The dangers facing the species are development on the shores of the lagoons where it breeds and the increased numbers of boats, particularly tourist boats, coming to watch the whales.

Surviving seals

The story of sealing is rather different from whaling. There has not been such a large investment nor such a sustained attack on the world's population. In the nineteenth century there were massive onslaughts on fur seals and some other species, but these dwindled as the stocks disappeared. The seals managed to survive and probably only the Caribbean monk seal has become extinct. Other seals held on and many have recovered well, including fur seals in the Antarctic and Alaska, and British grey seals. Others have been less fortunate. The Mediterranean monk seal is very rare (only 500 left) and the Hawaiian endangered.

Attention to the plight of seals has been focused on the annual hunt of harp seals. The white-furred pups (called 'whitecoats') are born on the ice off the eastern coasts of Canada, around Greenland, Jan Mayen and in the

White Sea and are killed in large numbers by clubbing. A heavy club is a humane weapon for killing thin-skulled seals, if used properly, but this hunt, or rather series of hunts, has attracted considerable public concern. Aside from the ethical question of seal hunts, there was no restriction on the number killed annually. Since 1971, however, quotas have been imposed in Canadian waters, in roughly the same manner as for whales. The quota for 1977 was 160,000 whitecoats with a ban on killing adults, and it seems that harp seal numbers are increasing. Hooded seal pups, called bluebacks, are very valuable. They are scattered over the pack ice so both hunting and research are more difficult. A quota of 15,000 was set in 1977, but it is not known for certain whether this is a suitable figure.

Dangers and disturbances

Hunting is not the most serious danger facing most species of seals. As with porpoises, many are caught in nets set for fish. They suffer from oil and other pollution of the sea and they suffer from disturbance, whether it is 'friendly' disturbance of tourists or 'hostile' disturbance by mindless marksmen. Competition with fishermen is all-important. Fishermen shoot seals that come too near their nets, but the huge increase of fishing

Because the monk seal is well disposed towards man it has been slaughtered relentlessly. The last-known West Indian monk seals were killed in 1911

around the world has robbed the seals of their food. The fur seals of the Pribilof islands had recovered from their near-destruction in the nineteenth century, but they are in decline again as trawler fleets have moved on to their feeding grounds.

Other sea mammals

Whales and seals steal the limelight in conservation circles and it is sometimes forgotten that there are other mammals living in the sea. These are the two sea cows (dugong and manatees), the sea otter and the polar bear. All have suffered considerably at the hands of man. The sea cows live in coastal waters or in estuaries, where they are easy to hunt for their meat. They are officially protected in many countries, but they often live in remote places, where law enforcement barely reaches. The sea otter is in a better position. Protection has allowed it to recover its numbers on the west coast of North America except where pollution and disturbance prevent recolonization. Polar bears seemed set to go the way of other sea mammals as increasing numbers were being hunted during the 1960s, often for sport. Then, in 1973, nations with Arctic territory (USA, USSR, Canada, Norway and Denmark) prohibited hunting except by locals.

A polar bear in the Canadian Arctic. These bears have been hunted just as ruthlessly as other sea mammals and were frequently shot from the air for sport

Bluefin tuna: *conserving a dwindling resource*

The largest of the marine food fishes, the most widespread and a fish capable of extensive migrations, is the bluefin tuna, also known as the great or common tunny, sometimes as the horse mackerel, confusingly so since this is an alternative name for the unrelated scad. The bluefin tuna was first made the object of an organized fishery by the Phoenicians, off the coast of Spain. Its salted flesh was much esteemed by the Romans under the name *Saltamentum sardicum* and from those days on there has been a traditional tunny fishery in the Mediterranean and Black seas. In about 1900 the Spanish name, tuna, appears to have come into use in California and today this name, for the flesh of this giant member of the mackerel family, is a household word on both sides of the Atlantic as well as across the North American continent.

Migration evidence

Although the tuna has such a long and honourable history its biology is relatively little-known. Tagging has shown it capable of migrating from the Florida Straits eastwards to Norway and the Bay of Biscay and southwards to the seas off southern Argentina. There was also a flourishing fishery off South Africa until 1970. It was not until 1963 that the first positive evidence was obtained of migration across the Pacific, with populations of bluefins in both the Kuroshio Current off Japan and the California Current. The tuna gather in the Kuroshio Current in February south of Japan and migrate northwards in spring, returning in the autumn. On the eastern side they appear off Baja California in June, move northwards to California by September and are occasionally found as far north as Oregon, Washington and Alaska. They return to the Kuroshio area to spawn.

Tuna boom

The tuna-fishing industry is one of the more recent developments in high-sea fisheries. As with other marine resources there has been a marked boom in the middle years of the present century. As a result there has been increasing concern, in the fishing industry itself and among scientists, that the bluefin in both Mediterranean and Atlantic waters was reaching a dangerously low level. Against the 40,000 metric tons taken in the Atlantic in the early 1960s, the yield had dropped to 13,000 metric tons in 1972 and 1973. Added to the traditional fisheries in Europe, the boom in American use of tuna was quickly followed by the demand for large bluefin tuna for the sashimi (raw fish market) in Japan. Dockside prices for these giant fish, with a firm flesh excelling that of the sturgeon for palatability, rose to two dollars a pound.

Already, in 1970, the decline in tuna stocks off southwest Africa, where Japanese ships had taken a heavy toll, had been highlighted. Between 1964 and 1967 two million tuna had been taken, mainly longfin tuna, with yellowfin tuna a poor second, but the catch had also included bluefins as well as big-eye tuna. The longfins were by then so depleted that it was not economic to fish for them and attention was directed to the other species. The southwest Africa statistics show how readily overfishing can reduce the stocks as well as indicating another area in the Atlantic to which bluefins are known to migrate.

The Japanese used long lines, which is only one of the several methods used on tuna. Another is the purse seine net, used in the Pacific; and the oldest of all is the madrague, used in the Mediterranean. In the madrague the tuna are guided by long nets hung in the sea that lead the fish into a

Tuna-fishing in the Mediterranean. The huge fish are guided into a net chamber and then speared or clubbed before being hauled aboard

chamber formed by a stouter net. This is then closed and the tuna clubbed or speared. Then there is the sophisticated sport-fishing equipment used along the east coast of the United States and Canada.

In 1969 the International Commission for the Conservation of Atlantic Tuna met in Rome, under the aegis of the Food and Agriculture Organization, to consider what international action could be taken to conserve tuna stocks in the Atlantic. In 1974 the United States delegation to the ICCAT proposed that management measures should be adopted to conserve a dwindling resource, and that these should be Atlantic-wide,

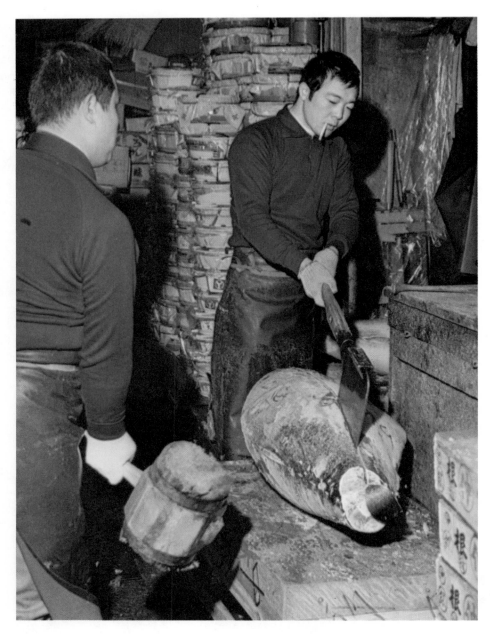

Cutting up tuna. The Japanese are responsible for more tuna-fishing than any other country

involving not only the United States and Canada but also France, Spain, Morocco and Japan. The regulations drawn up went into force in 1975. In general, also, research programmes were drawn up that included tagging to study the movements of the fish, the maintenance of catch logs and other measures likely to produce information that might help in restoring the bluefin to its former level of abundance. Sport fishermen were invited to co-operate.

Young heavily exploited

A first result was to show a decline throughout the Atlantic with dramatic changes in the size composition in the various populations. The main spawning areas are in the Gulf of Mexico and in the Florida Straits, between the mid-Atlantic states and Bermuda, in the Mediterranean, the Black Sea and the Gulf of Guinea. At four months old the young tuna weigh around half a pound. At one year this has increased to nine pounds, the weight being doubled for each of the next three years of age, when the fish are becoming sexually mature. Recovery of tagged individuals has

Loading tuna by hand on the Mediterranean coast. This popular fish has been victim of extremely heavy exploitation

revealed that the age groups one to five years were being heavily exploited, so repeating the familiar sequence of 'eating the seed corn'.

Sport-fishing paradox

A seeming paradox emerged in the statistics for the Bahamas. The average weight of bluefins caught in sport-fishing in the 1950s was 450 pounds. In the early 1970s it was 580 pounds and this had increased to 645 pounds in 1976. Maximum sizes caught showed a similar trend. In the Bahamas, in 1976, two 900-pounders were landed where previously 700 pounds was reckoned large, and whereas the world record had long been under 1000 pounds in 1970 a 1065-pound bluefin was recorded to be beaten by 1120 pounds in 1973, while two years later thirty-nine bluefins of over 1000 pounds were caught in Canadian waters alone.

The occurrence of individuals of unusually large size would seem to indicate success in a species. In tuna it indicates a drastic thinning of the population leaving more food, in the shape of small fishes, for the survivors, in which growth is accelerated accordingly.

Krill: *huge potential harvest*

The world's trawler fleets are continually searching for new fishing grounds. Apart from the growing need to expand food supplies, many of the traditional fishing grounds have been grossly over-exploited. The Southern Ocean, which encircles the continent of Antarctica, has barely been appreciated as a fishing ground until recent years. It is a vast tract of ice-bound and stormy seas that has already seen two waves of commercial exploitation.

Hard on the heels of discovery of land at the southern end of the Atlantic Ocean in the latter stages of the eighteenth century, sealers poured down from North America and European ports to hunt for seals. It did not take them many years to destroy the seal herds. Then, in the twentieth century, it was the turn of the great whales. Now, in the 1970s, Antarctic whaling has become barely profitable, but it has been realized that the Southern Ocean swarms with many different kinds of fish, squid and other forms of marine life, which offer a massive potential fishery. The most important of these forms is krill, a two inch, shrimp-like crustacean.

The head of a single krill specimen. Krill swim by means of five pairs of paddles beneath the abdomen and trap plankton with the feathery appendages of the fore-parts of the body

Frozen krill being removed from a horizontal plate freezer on a factory ship in the Antarctic. It is very possible that in future krill will be processed and be used as a food additive

As yet, the life history of krill is not fully known. Shoals have been caught at depths of 1300 feet, but eggs have been found at 6500 feet. The eggs are laid at the surface in late summer, then sink. After hatching, the larvae swim to the surface and then take around two years to develop into the adult form. During this time, they are carried in shoals around and about in ocean currents. Some of these shoals are enormous. They measure hundreds of yards across and contain hundreds of tons of krill. They play a very important role in the Southern Ocean as they are the main food for many animals.

Whales specially equipped

Krill are the almost exclusive food of the Antarctic great whales, whose mouths are equipped with a fringe of baleen plates for straining small animals from the sea. It has been estimated that, before the numbers of Antarctic whales were reduced by hunting, they ate 150 million tons of krill every year. With the destruction of the whale stocks, the present consumption is probably about forty-three million tons. Yet whales are only one group of animals out of many to eat krill. Of the 500 million tons of krill which are produced in the Southern Ocean each year, sixty-four million tons are eaten by seals, five to eight and a half million tons by sea birds (including penguins and albatrosses) and an unknown but vast tonnage by fish and squid. Whether these animals compete for krill is not known for certain, but the numbers of fur seals and crabeater seals have increased since the whales became rare. This suggests that there is now more food for them and it is possible that these burgeoning seal populations may prevent the whales from recovering their abundance by denying them food.

The difference between past and present estimates of the annual consumption of krill by whales is in the order of 100 million tons. For comparison, the total world catch of fish is around seventy million tons, so there is a huge potential harvest which could go a long way to solving the world's food problems. Several nations are engaged in investigating the possibilities of fishing for krill. They have made large catches using modern trawlers equipped with echolocation equipment, but the main problem is economic. The krill has to be turned into a commercial, edible product.

Useful food additive

The Japanese and Russians have already marketed krill paste for enriching soups and stews and it seems likely that the best marketing policy is to use krill as an additive like soya bean flour or fish meal. Unfortunately, there is little chance of vast quantities of krill being used to stave off starvation in the Third World. Fishing for krill is an expensive business involving the latest and largest trawlers and skilled crews. Processing is also expensive and the operation is viable only if krill products command a good price. The present likelihood is that krill-harvesting will benefit underdeveloped countries indirectly. Krill will be used as an additive, or even canned, by the developed nations, thereby reducing the need to import other foods from poorer countries.

A mass of freshly caught krill; shrimp-like crustaceans of about two inches in length. The dark colour is partly due to the fact that they have guts full of diatoms

Porpoise: *accidental victims*

The high mortality among dolphins and porpoises through the yellowfin tuna fishery was highlighted by Dr William F. Perrin, in 1970, at a conference in California on biological sonar and diving mammals. The tuna associate with dolphins and porpoises, but while the tuna are below the surface and not easy to see, the dolphins and porpoises must surface to 'blow'. This guides the tuna fishers to the shoals. When these are sighted, the tuna vessels send out small speedboats to cast their seine nets, enclosing porpoises and tuna alike.

Part of the catch

The porpoises mainly involved are the spotted porpoise and the spinner or spinning porpoise. The common porpoise is encountered less frequently. Once the two ends of the seine net have been brought together, the problem arises as to how to get rid of the porpoises without losing the catch of tuna. As a rule, the problem is solved by lowering the net at one end, so allowing the porpoises to leap it. Another method is to wait until one half of the net has been hauled aboard, then backing and turning the boat to spill the porpoises over the top of the net.

The problem is complicated by the different behaviour of the two

Porpoises swim together and form schools of as many as several hundred. Sometimes as much as fifty per cent of a school caught in a tuna net will die

species most commonly caught in the net. The spinners, so named for their habit of leaping at times out of the sèa and spinning in mid-air before dropping back into the water, tend to panic and become entangled in the net. Then they cannot surface to breathe and are drowned. Even the spotted porpoises, which remain relatively calm, often get entangled and drown quickly because, except when cruising leisurely, they need to surface six to twelve times a minute to breath.

Damage and death

Not all skippers of tuna vessels are prepared to go to the trouble of trying to free the porpoises, with the result that as much as fifty per cent of a school caught in the net die, many more are injured and probably die later. Even the disruption to a school, caused by its being encircled, may result in death and injuries not immediately apparent to the onlookers. Dr Perrin reported to the conference that one fishing boat he accompanied in 1966, in catching 300 tons of tuna, brought about the known deaths of 2000 porpoises. Another statistic he gave, for 1969, was of a tuna boat which in fifteen net-sets, in the course of a month, caused a known total of 1697 porpoises to be killed in catching 312 tons of tuna. The porpoises killed in any one operation may be as low as one per cent of the school or as high as fifty per cent, with an average of just over five porpoises killed for every ton

Below: porpoises, with their large brains, have been subject to much experimentation. This photo shows 'Kathy' whose 'second sight' is being studied. Blindfolded, she finds her way through close-set poles; her sonar system pinpoints them exactly, although she cannot see

Right: porpoises are renowned for their 'human' qualities

Left: diver and porpoise show mutual interest for each other. Highly intelligent, porpoises tend to be inquisitive

of fish taken. Since yellowfin tuna-fishing has an annual haul of 45,000 tons this gives a probable total of not less than 244,000 porpoises needlessly exterminated each year.

By 1974 it was reported that although most tuna boats were equipped with the Medina net, which helps to prevent the drowning of porpoises and dolphins, the loss among porpoises was around 300,000 in 1971, and nearly 400,000 in 1972. This was because there had been an increase in yellowfin-fishing. The total actually netted in 1973 was given as one and a half million. The United States Marine Mammals Commission began to take a tough line. It also declared that the National Marine Fisheries Service research programme was inadequate.

Threats and violence

The Marine Mammal Protection Act of 1972 requires that such killing be reduced to insignificant levels, approaching zero. Then some of the tuna skippers became angry with the observers acting on behalf of the National Marine Fisheries Service, threatening violence, even murder. The path of conservation, like the alleged path of true love, is not always smooth. The government gave way and, quite illegally, decided not to enforce the law, while ninety per cent of the tuna boats were, apparently, violating it, with no hint of prosecutions. Meanwhile, nations other than the United States were taking no action with their fishing fleets. So ships other than those flying the United States flag could fish with impunity. Inevitably, American boat owners began to look for ways and means of operating under flags of other nationalities, if only to play for safety.

Conservative estimate

In 1976 the World Wildlife Fund estimated that between five and seven million porpoises and dolphins had died from this cause alone in the previous twenty years. This was almost certainly a conservative estimate. The Fund urged the Inter-American Tropical Tuna Commission, as well as its member governments (Canada, Costa Rica, Panama, Mexico, Nicaragua, France and the United States) to press forward vigorously with its plan to devise new equipment and fishing techniques to obviate the carnage among these sea mammals.

The latest reports tell of a porpoise-releasing tuna net having been designed which it is hoped will provide a solution to the problem. The net separates the tuna in a lower net while the porpoises collect in the upper net, from which they can be easily removed.

Among the fastest of marine animals, porpoises can reach a speed of twenty-five knots in pursuit of fish for food

Sea monster: *prehistoric monster or huge shark?*

There is a simple story, from years ago, of how some people living in a remote village came across something lying in the grass that they could not identify. They were half afraid to touch it. Then someone thought of old Ebenezer, the village wiseacre, so off they went to fetch him. When they had wheeled old Uncle Eb to the spot he looked at the object musingly, then cleared his throat and asked them to wheel him round it so that he could take a better look. After that he seemed to go into a trance. Then he cleared his throat again. 'Why, it's a thingmabob', he pronounced hesitatingly, 'a whatsitsname'. For a few more moments he contemplated the object once more. 'Of course, dang me', he declared triumphantly, 'it's a clickmadoodle'.

Even in the sophisticated times in which we are living, the same kind of thing takes place, especially over large animals seen in water or taken from water. A good example occurred in July 1977 when a Japanese fishing vessel, the Zuiyo Maru, was trawling off New Zealand. From a depth of 900 feet the trawl brought up a stinking carcase. It was said to be thirty feet long with a six-foot tail and was said to weigh two tons. We are told the 'creature' was sketched and photographed before the skipper ordered the unwholesome mass to be cast back into the sea for fear it might pollute the normal catch.

Similar to plesiosaur

Mr Michihiko Yano, an official of the Japanese fisheries company, who was on board and who took the photographs, expressed regret later that no attempt had been made to collect a few of the bones. He estimated that the animal must have been dead about a month, that most of the flesh was gone, that the internal organs were missing and that the lower jaw had fallen away. The rib cage was, however, declared to have been intact and clearly visible. The description given of the carcase was that it was 'like a snake with a turtle's body and front and rear flippers', which is very near the classic description of the extinct reptile known as a plesiosaur.

As soon as the fisheries company heard about the find they ordered all their ships in New Zealand waters to search for the carcase, but without success. So, as has happened so often before, the event was wide open to speculation with virtually no solid fact on which to base an identification. The mysterious object brought up in the trawl now became the prey of the Old Uncle Ebs of press and radio, who pronounced it a plesiosaur, a sea monster, a prehistoric fish, and extinct reptile (unspecified).

Mr Toshio Shickama, palaeontologist at Yokohama University, was reported as saying: 'There is no known sea creature existing like the one in Mr Yano's photographs'. He took the view that it could not be a type of fish or even a mammoth seal because it was much too big and had too long a neck. His guess was that it could have been a reptile related to the plesiosaur.

Several so-called sea monsters have been reported from various parts of the world and the descriptions of them, and the photographs, where these have been taken, show an intriguing similarity. All appear to consist of a rounded body, a long thin neck ending in a small head, a long tail and four flippers. They all have a length of about thirty feet, and there are three fishes that go to this length. One is the great white shark found in all warm waters of the world, occasionally straying into temperate waters. It can grow to thirty-six feet or more. Another is the basking shark, which is forty

The deception can be readily explained. As the carcase rots the first part to fall away is the skeleton of the jaws and gill arches, the bulkiest part of the head. This leaves the cranium, shaped like a snake's head, and the front part of the vertebral column looking like a long thin neck. The flesh of the tail also is soon lost, exposing the end of the vertebral column. This leaves the flesh of the body proper and the pectoral and pelvic fins, looking like two pairs of flippers, recalling those of a plesiosaur. Much depends on the degree of rotting. In fact, the mass of putrefying material can take so many forms that endless phantasmagoria can be conjured up

feet or more long, found in temperate seas in both hemispheres, and especially in the North Atlantic. The third is the whale shark, not often seen, but recorded sporadically from the warm oceanic waters of the world. It may grow to a length of fifty feet or more.

Occasionally the carcase, particularly of the basking shark, is cast ashore, usually on some inaccessible rocky, storm-bound coast. There it is found by an Old Uncle Eb, who manages to give a fanciful account of what he has seen. The most famous is the so-called Monster of Stronsay, cast ashore on the Orkney islands at the beginning of the nineteenth century. It was actually described in a learned journal as an unknown species of animal and given the scientific name of *Halsydrus pontoppidiani*. Fortunately a few vertebrae were collected and preserved and subsequent examination showed these to be the bones of a basking shark. Others have been variously described as sea monsters and sea serpents.

At least one trained zoologist was misled until he made a detailed examination and left no doubt of his 'sea serpent' being no more than the rotting carcase of a large shark.

The body of the Zuiyo Maru monster is gone beyond recall, and the interest it aroused has largely died down. It is significant that a few fragments of it that were salvaged have been pronounced as 'shark', but whether great white, basking or whale shark is probably beyond deciding.

Fish: *decline of a marine harvest*

In mankind's rape of the environment nothing, in the air, on the land or in the fresh waters, can exceed the devastation of the sea. Its effects are less spectacular only because, being primarily land-dwellers, we make, as a species, less contact with this vast volume of salt water than with the other parts of our environment, although the seas and oceans together cover two-thirds of the surface of the earth. They are less spectacular also because what is happening lies below the surface and a panoramic viewing of it cannot be made. If, however, we take the species one by one we can build an adequate picture, especially from the sizes of commercial catches.

Marine abundance

The herring, more perhaps than any other species of fish, underlines the abundance of marine life. Ten years ago 3000 million herrings were taken from the sea annually around the North Atlantic. Before 1914 a million tons were landed at British ports on the North Sea and slightly more were landed for the rest of Europe. Fishing for herrings in an organized way has been going on in Europe since the Middle Ages, 900–600 years ago. It first comes into prominence in the rise of the Hanseatic League, centred around the German towns of Hamburg, Rostock and Lübeck. The herrings they traded came from the Baltic and in the middle of the fifteenth century, for no known reason, the Baltic herring disappeared. Then came the turn of the Dutch to harvest the North Sea herring, leading to conflict with Great Britain.

The North Sea herring fishery fluctuated between 1915 and 1927, with a good brood hatched every three years. After that the fluctuations became less regular until in 1930 came a disastrous year. The stocks recovered to some extent, but then came a change in the fishery itself. Instead of the thousand or more drifters working from British ports, the number is now only a few hundred. Britain formerly exported most of its catch to Germany and Russia. Today Germany has its own herring fishery, so has Russia, and Japanese ships have come on to the scene. Because herring fishing is now shared by so many nations it is difficult to obtain the

Below: pulling in a sardine catch in Natal, South Africa. The whole area possesses a great wealth of fish, which has been tapped only in recent times

necessary data that would tell us the state of the herring stocks. There is, nevertheless, a general impression of a declining industry.

Any drop in numbers of the herring shoals may be due to overfishing or it may, like the Baltic herring's disappearance, be incapable of explanation. Professor Otto Pettersson, the Swedish hydrographer, claims to have found evidence for a fluctuation in oceanological factors over a period of 1800 years and he linked this with the abundance of herrings in 600–400 BC and again in the Middle Ages, AD 1000–1400. If correct, this could mean we are in a recession and that herrings will once again become abundant in AD 2800–3200.

Stormy cod career

The career of the Atlantic cod has been almost as stormy as that of the herring, ending in the 'cod war' of the 1970s between Iceland and Britain. Cod was caught and salted or dried in prehistoric times and in the Middle Ages it was given the name of 'stockfish', a common item of diet. It has also been used as a source of glue, from its skin, of isinglass, a gelatin and purifying agent, obtained from the swim bladder, and cod liver oil for medicinal purposes. But mainly it is in demand for its flesh, boiled or steamed, as fish sticks or, in Britain, the main ingredient of fish-and-chips.

Around Greenland, where cod had always been found in abundance, stocks began to decline in the early 1960s. Iceland, whose national economy depends eighty per cent on fishing, began to fear that its stocks might be in danger. This caused her to extend her fishing limits from eighteen to fifty miles from her coast, leading to the 'cod war' with Britain, in which the British trawlers had their wires cut, had warning shots fired across their bows or were rammed by Icelandic gunboats. Finally the British government sent its own gunboats in to protect the trawlers.

It is understandable that the British cod-fishers should wish to retain rights they had been exercising for many years. Equally understandable are the anxieties of the Icelanders that their national livelihood may be in jeopardy. Until almost the middle of this century cod-fishing depended on the skill and judgement of the skipper and his crew. Today, sonar and other electronic equipment can be used to locate the fish and, as in Iceland, land-based planes can be used to spot the fish and call the waiting crews to

Below: the netters gather the fish into baskets

Below right: the baskets are then tipped on to the sand

Untold damage can be caused by man's carelessness. This is an aerial view of an acid waste dump off the New York/New Jersey coast. The elongated blue patch is the dump and the greenish area to the southwest is the acid mixing with water

the fishing grounds. A single sweep of the trawl may net 15,000 pounds of fish, mainly cod.

Statistics must also be disquieting to the Icelanders. There has been an increasing number of ships from more countries than formerly, including Britain, Canada, France, Germany, Poland, Portugal, Romania and Spain and also the USSR and Japan; the last two taking a greater share than any of the others, with their large fleets of factory ships.

The average weight of the individual cod taken in 1970 was around five pounds, giving an approximate figure of just over a thousand million cod taken from the sea in one year. A female cod may lay up to seven million eggs in one year, compared with up to 50,000 by the herring, but of these at most ten eggs laid will survive the many hazards and predators to develop into mature fish.

Oldest fisheries

The world's oldest organized fisheries are those located in the North Atlantic based over the continental shelf of Europe, Iceland, Greenland and the Atlantic seaboard of northeastern North America. They concern primarily the herring and the cod. There is a similar ecosystem in the North Pacific based on the continental shelf that runs from the Sea of Japan under the Bering Sea to the Gulf of Alaska. The species of fishes involved are different from those in the North Atlantic, although one of them, the Pacific pollock, *Theragra chalcogramma*, is a member of the cod family and the Pacific counterpart of the Atlantic cod *Gadus morhua*.

Wise conservation

Within this Pacific area, which was exploited later than that of the North Atlantic, events have presented us with two textbook examples of conservation, the one illustrating the effects of wise management, the other illustrating the results of unwise action. The first concerns the Pribilof fur seal, which lives dispersed across the North Pacific, but uses the Pribilof islands, off the coast of Alaska, as a breeding ground. The story of the Pribilof seal is a familiar one, but its outline can be recalled. The seal was over-exploited by the sealers so that its original population of several million was reduced, in the early years of this century, to a few hundred thousand leading to the species being on the brink of extinction. Then, by what can only be regarded as a brilliant stroke by American biologists, it was saved in an exercise that can stand for all time as the prototype of eating your cake while still preserving it. The first step was to give total protection to the seal. Then, by killing a specified number each year of surplus non-breeding males, the so-called bachelor males, a harvest of fur skins could be reaped which at the same time allowed the total population to increase (see Sea mammal article).

Useful casualties

This seeming paradox was brought about by the realization that the young, unmated males fought among themselves and with the breeding males, producing casualties. In a completely natural state, prior to the intervention of man the sealer, this had provided the natural check on overpopulation. So in acting on the recommendations of the biologists who studied the problem, the natural check was substituted by an unnatural check, which achieved the same result, but provided at the same time a supply of fur skins for the world market, which would, under the natural process, have lain on the beaches of the Pribilofs and rotted.

The lesson learned has been applied elsewhere, to other species of seals, and to animal species other than seals. The underlying principle is perhaps even more important: that species can be preserved, as well as being utilized

Below: the cod end of a bottom trawl being emptied. The catch is ice fish, a food fish that has only been used as such recently as cod stocks decline

Below left: cod, grey sole and squid being processed at a fishing products factory

if a thorough study is made of their biology in the first instance.

The second example from the North Pacific illustrates the reverse. When the Japanese and Russian fleets first began to operate in a big way in the Bering Sea, in the late 1950s, their primary target was the yellowfin sole. Today, the Japanese fisheries account for the world's largest landings of seafoods, supplying half their country's consumption of animal protein. Prior to 1960 there came into operation in the Bering Sea a Japanese fleet of a dozen factory ships, known as mother-ships, each with a dozen attendant trawlers. In addition were forty or more independent trawlers. The catch of yellowfin sole rose from a previous 100,000–200,000 metric tons annually to more than 400,000 metric tons. Then the numbers fell drastically. To such a rapacious fleet, fishing the yellowfin sole had now become uneconomic. So the Japanese, joined by the Russians, who had been operating similar fleets, also equipped with electronic devices that increased the efficiency of their fishing, turned to the Pacific pollock.

Factory farming

The importance of these composite fleets is that the catches from the trawlers are transferred to the factory ship, where they are processed. The products are collected from the factory ships by large cargo vessels, which also bring food and other supplies. So the composite fleets can remain at sea for months on end, cutting out the long journeys to and from the fishing ground, as in more orthodox fishing methods.

Pollock brought to a low ebb

The Pacific pollock has been described as the most abundant fish species used for human consumption. If that statement is justified then the species exceeded in abundance the vast shoals of cod and herring, which showed signs of becoming depleted, apart from the Baltic herring, only after centuries of exploitation by many nations. The pollock was brought to a low ebb in little more than a decade. The United States had traditionally drawn upon the Atlantic cod as an inexpensive source of fish products, but in 1973 increased its catch of pollock from 800 metric tons in 1971 to 20,000 metric tons. This is a modest figure beside the increased catch of Russian trawlers which leapt from 60,000 metric tons to 300,000 metric tons in 1972. Even this was less than half the toll taken by the Japanese

Below left: a catch of sprats

Below: a school of snappers, Crystal river, Florida. Snappers live in large schools numbering billions and are important food fish in many tropical regions

Right: a variety of sea foods being fished off Scotland

Below: a school of herrings off the New Hebrides. The herring has been fished in an organized way in Europe since the Middle Ages

fleet, which had been increasing its catch by up to thirty per cent each year to one point five million metric tons.

One of the first effects of overfishing is that the size of the fish caught begins to decline. At first sixteen-inch pollock were being caught. By 1974 eighty per cent of the Japanese catch were twelve inches long. The Pacific pollock matures at three to four years of age and a length of sixteen inches. So not only were more fish being taken out of the sea, there were increasingly fewer immatures to replace the mature fish that had been, or were being, taken. There comes a point when the toll of fish being harvested exceeds the annual recruitment to the stock and, unless fishing pressure is eased, there is a catastrophic fall in numbers. It had happened with the yellowfin sole; it was happening now with the pollock. When fishing is international only international action can retrieve the situation. In 1973 the Japanese, realizing what was happening, shortened their fishing season from ten months to nine and took other measures. In 1974, in co-operation with the United States, they agreed to reduce their catch still further. The Russians were less co-operative.

Natural adverse factors

In a situation of this kind complete cessation of fishing could result in the stocks being fully replenished in a few years, the time taken depending on how long is necessary for the remaining young to mature and breed. The danger is ever present of a natural adverse factor intervening that could administer a *coup de grâce* before the natural regeneration could take effect. It appears that something of this sort is occurring in the pollock's feeding grounds. Japanese oceanographers found that since 1970 Arctic water persisted in summer over a larger part of the Bering Sea area than in the 1960s. This brought a drop of several degrees in the temperature of the sea. This could be more damaging than overfishing, but the two combined could cause either a virtual disappearance of the pollock or a shift of its population to a more southerly area.

Right: young bass, 'seedcorn' that will one day grow into sport-fish with highly palatable flesh. They are sometimes caught in fishermens' nets

Below right: a Russian factory ship with trawlers alongside, off the Shetland Isles

Below: barracuda. The consumption of fish, like other things, is often governed by fashion, and at present people regard 'strange' fish with trepidation. The sea is full of a mass of unfamiliar fish, which could in fact be eaten. Barracuda are ugly and ferocious, but they are eaten on the California coast

MISCELLANY

Albinism   Animal dreams   Chimpanzee
Animal tool-users   Bluebird   Sociobiology   Alaska pipeline

This final section is a miscellany of unrelated topics that have all aroused considerable interest in the past few years.

Albinism has always fascinated man and occurs frequently in animal and bird species. When Chris McBride discovered two white lion cubs in Timbavati curiosity was aroused world wide. This article discusses the various different kinds of albinism.

Dog- and cat-owners have often claimed that their animals dream, and until very recently the idea has always been rejected by scientists. After experiments and investigation it has now been established that not only is it acceptable that animals dream but that it is essential for them to do so.

Communication between animals has long been acknowledged and there has been much speculation as to whether chimpanzees, so like humans, are capable of communicating with us. The Lana Language Project was set up in which a chimpanzee was able to communicate via a computer and the results of this study have enabled scientists to reach several firm conclusions on this fascinating subject.

Since the recognition that the digger wasp is an animal tool-user, numerous animals and birds have been found to be using tools in as many different ways. Tool-using, as we all know, makes life easier for us and, it seems, for animals and birds as well.

The American bluebird, although a great favourite with man, has been an unfortunate victim of man's tidying up of the habitat. In order to rectify the situation a network of 'bluebird trails' has been set up across the continent.

A new subject in the study of animal life has been devised. Sociobiology, a cross between biology and natural history, is the study of the animal's social behaviour, and how its society is organized—many fascinating observations have been made.

Alaska, rich in mineral resources, is commonly thought of as being a vast barren wasteland. When it was decided to transport its oil by pipeline overland, it was realized that wildlife would be seriously disrupted. Careful plans and studies are needed if disruption of the unique wildlife and environment of this area is to be kept to a minimum.

An albino blackbird

Albinism: *the fascination of white animals*

The Timbavati reserve is one of fifteen private nature reserves on South Africa's Low Veldt. It has an area of 208 square miles within which are fifteen so-called farms, tracts of wild bush, uncultivated and teeming with wildlife, including lions. It was in one of these in October 1975 that Chris McBride first saw his white lions, two white cubs of a litter that included a tawny, normally coloured cub. As McBride pointed out, white lions are something of a legend in Africa, just as white elephants are in southeast Asia. The white lions of Timbavati received much publicity and a book has been written about them.

For a reason, hard to define, whiteness in animals that are otherwise normally coloured, seems to hold an unusual attraction for us. The white elephant, for example, is held sacred and may not be worked, so anyone possessing a white elephant finds himself burdened with a beast of enormous appetite that needs to be fed and tended for up to seventy years, the maximum life-span of the Asiatic elephant. So we refer to any useless object about the house as a white elephant.

Mystery whiteness

Whiteness in animals is still something of a mystery. In virtually every species except those in which colour is due to structure of the surface, as in insects, there can occur individuals that are completely lacking black pigment. They are white all over except for pink eyes and skin. The colour of the eyes is governed by that of the blood in the retina seen through the transparent lens. The pink colour of the skin is also due to the colour of the blood showing through. These are true albinos. Some species seem to produce albinos more frequently than other species, but in all they are rare, perhaps one in a hundred thousand, more commonly one in a million or more. Albinism is a hereditary factor, and this, together with the

Much interest has been generated by Chris McBride's discovery and studies of the albino lions at the Timbavati Private Nature Reserve

statement that it is caused by a total lack of pigment, is about all that can be said with any degree of certainty.

Partial albinos

As well as true, or total, albinos there are partial albinos. These are more common. As with true albinos, the ratio of partial albinos to normally coloured individuals in any species varies considerably. One in which partial albinism is so frequent as to call forth no surprise in a knowledgeable ornithologist is the European blackbird. Such a bird may be normally coloured except for a white collar or a patch of white on the head, back, wing or tail. In extreme examples the blackbird may be speckled white over its entire body. That the condition is inherited can be seen where a partial albino blackbird sires a brood in which the offspring are normally coloured except for one or two that have patches of white on them. As its descendants themselves increase and breed, the partial albinism spreads through the district in the years that follow and then gradually dies out, over a period of perhaps ten years, after which all blackbirds in the neighbourhood are seen to be normally coloured once more.

Whiteness that is not regarded as albinism or partial albinism is seen in such animals as swans, which have a pure white plumage except as cygnets, and furred animals or birds, such as the ermine or ptarmigan, that are coloured in summer, white in winter.

Colour variation

There is another kind of whiteness arising from a different cause, from the tendency of all individuals within a species to vary in colour. Among Caucasians, usually referred to as 'white people', there may be blondes and brunettes and redheads, even within one family. This variation follows the complex laws of heredity, as indeed do albinism and partial albinism, but, unlike those two, colour variation is an everyday phenomenon, of which we take little conscious notice until a discussion such as this is embarked

Two Manchurian tigers at Delhi Zoo, India. Unlike many other kinds of albino, this species retains its characteristic markings quite vividly

upon. It is the same with animals. In the tiger, for example, the Manchurian tiger has a pale background for its stripes, while the Bengal tiger, merely another subspecies of the species *Panthera tigris*, has a rich red-tawny coat with intense brown-black stripes. Yet in 1911, King George V of Britain, on a visit to India, shot a white tiger in Bengal, pure white with pale brown stripes.

The variations in colour of the African lion range from pale sandy to a rich tawny, with a tawny mane; or the mane may be black (or absent altogether). All such variations are no more significant than the colour varieties of hair seen in 'white' races of man, from jet black hair, dark eyes and a swarthy skin to the blonde or even the extreme blonde in which the hair is almost pure white, even in youth, the eyes pale blue or grey and the skin milky pale. Like albinism these variations are genetically based.

Melanism

The reverse of albinism is melanism, when there is an excess of melanin, the black pigment. The best-known example is the black panther, a black variety of the leopard. Albinos suffer the disadvantage that they are readily seen by their enemies. The relatively high proportion of black leopards may be because leopards tend to live in forests and black leopards would be inconspicuous in the shade.

Another colour peculiarity is that known as the colour phase. The golden cat of southeast Asia comes in two phases, reddish or grey, either unspotted or with conspicuous spots and blotches. The African tiger cat may be red or grey and may change from one to the other at the moult.

An albino Indian elephant is shown here on the right along with a normally coloured one. In Thailand the white elephant is believed to contain the soul of Buddha and is baptized, feted and mourned for at its death at up to seventy years of age

Right: used a great deal for experiments in laboratories and kept as pets white rats are commonplace albinos

Below: the black panther a variety of leopard is the best-known example of melanism

Animal dreams: *acceptable and essential*

Owners of dogs and cats have long stoutly maintained that their pets dream and they have continued to do so despite denials of scientists. Now, it seems, the two parties are united, for not only is it now scientifically acceptable that animals dream, but that it is essential they should do so.

A first step in settling this argument was taken when William Dement noticed that when babies are asleep their eyes make small movements. These are especially noticeable in babies because the bulge of the cornea pushes up the eyelid. The same movements occur in adults, at fairly regular intervals throughout the night. The rapid eye movements are known as REMs. The next step was to awaken people when making these REMs. They reported that they were dreaming, whereas anyone awakened when not making REMs reported they were not dreaming. From this it became possible to answer many other questions. It was possible, also, to carry the investigations to animals, which make similar REMs.

Effects of broken dreams

Another line of investigation was with two groups of sleepers, one of which was used as a control group. In the experimental group the sleeper would be roused as soon as REMs started, then letting the subject fall asleep again, but rousing him once more as soon as the REMs started afresh, so depriving him of his dreams. Members of the control group were wakened for the same amount of time, but during non-dream periods. Whereas members of the control group showed only the slight irritation resulting from having their sleep disturbed, those deprived of dreams began, after about a week, to show psychological disturbances.

Brain, the computer

Sleep, therefore, is not merely a restorative to tired muscles, it also provides a period during which our computer, the brain, can be updated and its programmes revised, as in a mechanical computer. The brain is not switched off during sleep, otherwise we should not have the common experience of going to bed with an apparently insoluble problem and waking the following morning with the complete answer to it.

What made pet owners so convinced that animals dream was their observation of those moments when a dog or cat, fast asleep, suddenly becomes active without waking. Its whiskers twitch, its paws and tail move, there are slight convulsions in the body and the animal breathes irregularly instead of rhythmically. Often these movements are accompanied by vocalizations: grunts, growls, mewings or other sounds appropriate to the species. In extreme cases a dog, for example, may give the impression, while curled up on the rug, of bounding through undergrowth, barking, as if hunting, except that all movements and sounds are less than life-size.

Animal surprise

Another comparison that can be made between human and animal sleepers is that when disturbed in the middle of a dreaming session they show surprise, even aggression. It is as though they are completely out of touch with their environment so that on being awakened they have passed from a strange (dream) world to the world of reality.

Studies have shown that the more complex the brain the greater learning ability and the greater is the need for dreaming to carry on the learning. Also, leaving aside hibernation, which is a special form of sleep, the more complex the brain possessed the greater the proportion of each twenty-four hours of each day that must be spent in sleep. Put another way, the more intelligent an animal the more sleep it needs. After man, the Primates (apes and monkeys) need most sleep and show more clearly REMs during sleep. Next in order come the carnivores, then the hoofed herbivores.

Dreaming birds

Birds also show indications of dreaming while asleep. This is most noticeable in parrots and the better 'talkers' they are, the more convincing is the evidence for it. Owners of parrots have reported how their pets, while asleep, will at times repeat the phrases they use when fully awake, but the words are jumbled, somewhat as the mental pictures we experience when dreaming are confused and, in a manner, nonsensical. Budgies and mynahs are also reported as talking in their sleep. Even reptiles are said to dream and apparently this is most striking in crocodiles. It is not so many decades ago that scientists awoke to the fact that fish sleep. Since then more and more evidence has been forthcoming to reinforce this idea. Some species go to particular places at night and there remain immobile, a few lying on their sides during the sleep period, and, most remarkable of all, certain parrotfishes not only go to a dormitory but put on the equivalent of a nightshirt, each parrotfish secreting an envelope of mucus around itself. In the morning it discards this and swims back to its feeding ground.

Speculation

Assuming that animals do truly dream, and that they do so in a manner strictly comparable with human dreams, the way is opened to an interesting line of speculation. Although our dreams are mainly a confused jumble of past experience there are also such things as precognitive dreams. One example is of a man who saw in his sleep the names of winners of horse races—making considerable financial gains as a consequence. There are many other, more serious, examples of future events apparently foretold in dreams. If animals can experience precognitive dreams, this could explain certain phenomena at present inexplicable, such as the dog that howls at the time of death of a person, the dog and the dying person being some distance apart at the time. This sounds like sheer fantasy, but so did the idea a few years ago of a bird or a crocodile dreaming.

Asleep and perhaps dreaming!
A mongrel puppy and a cat

Chimpanzee: *computer communication*

It has long been recognized that animals use a language to communicate with each other. In this social communication, as it should more strictly be called, one individual affects the behaviour of others by the transmission of stimuli that evoke responses. The stimuli may be gestural, vocal or chemical (as in scents and odours). Speech, by contrast, is a uniquely human form of language and even before serious study of animal language in the broader sense had begun, there were a few scientists who had turned their attention to the great apes. One tried to discover, by patient observation, whether gorillas 'talked' to each other and, if so, whether it was possible to learn their language and so communicate with them.

Limited success

It requires no unusual powers of perception to realize that the chimpanzee, gorilla and orang-utan are very like human beings in structure and in parts of their behaviour. Yet all efforts to teach apes to speak have met with limited success. Possibly the main reason is that the larynx of an ape lacks the specialized structure found in the human larynx. Then comes the thought that probably, in early man, the first exchanges were gestural.

At the beginning of the 1970s Beatrice T. Gardner and R. Allen Gardner, of the Psychology Department of the University of Nevada, published the surprising results of their researches. Using Washoe, a year-old chimpanzee, they had been able to demonstrate that at least one chimpanzee showed considerable facility to produce and apparently to understand the meaning of a number of words represented by the hand-produced signs of the American sign language for the deaf. In the initial stages she mastered only ten words, but these she began to string together in a rudimentary form of syntax. Eventually she developed a lexicon of more than 130 words.

Impressive word use

More impressive than learning the words was what she did with them. She was able, for example, to transfer signs to new referents. Thus, the word 'open' would be applied to any door and in due course to a refrigerator, drawer, box, jar, cupboard, briefcase and eventually to turning on a water faucet.

About the same time, another chimpanzee, Sarah, was being tested by David Premack of the University of Oklahoma. His methods entailed the use of plastic segments to represent words. These could be laid out in series to form simple sentences, such as 'Sarah take banana'. Later Sarah graduated to describing objects not present in the room. The segment for 'apple' was a piece of blue plastic yet Sarah was able to describe 'apple' as red, round and with a stem.

Recognition

R. Fouts, who studied with the Gardners, pursued language studies at the Institute of Primate Studies a few years later using Lucy, one of several chimpanzees. He was able to demonstrate further the ability of apes to recognize attributes of objects used. Thus, in due course, Lucy described four citrus fruits as 'smell fruits', radishes as 'cry hurt food', Brazil nuts as 'rock berries', ducks as 'water birds' (as in human speech!) and watermelons were aptly named 'drink fruit' and 'candy fruit'.

These successes stimulated Duane M. Rumbaugh, of the Yerkes Regional Primate Research Center of Emory University, Atlanta, Georgia, to contemplate using a computer-controlled training system. In

this he was joined by Timothy V. Gill in what was later called the Lana Language Project. They developed a language that could be accommodated by a relatively simple computer, with a chimpanzee, Lana, as the test subject.

Computerized language

A console was used with each key embossed with a geometric figure or lexigram representing a word. The keys were interchangeable to obviate the possibility of the ape learning their positions by rote, and they were arranged to give a six-word sentence, with a 'period' key that when depressed would mark the end of a sentence. Messages were recorded on a teleprinter and a paper-tape punch. A facsimile of each lexigram appeared on a projector above the console as each key was depressed, and below the console and under the control of the computer was an array of dispensers for vending requested foods and drinks and other objects, such as toys, a ball and a blanket. To the side of the console was a screen for projecting photographic slides or motion pictures. Also provided were systems that produced stereophonic music or opened a window to give a view out-of-doors, on request from Lana.

A similar console beyond the experimental chamber in which Lana lived made it possible for the experimenter to communicate with her by pressing a corresponding set of keys, the lexigram appearing on another row of projectors above her console. Thus there was two-way communication, and the facilities for question and answer between experimenter and subject. The computer system allowed for a twenty-four-hour working record to be kept without the experimenter being present at all times.

The language used was entirely visual and non-vocal and the inclusion of stereophonic music, the photographic slides, motion pictures and the view through the window was aimed at supplying an antidote to boredom for the ape. To avoid random use of the keys by the chimpanzee the keyboard was controlled by an overhead bar that needed to be depressed to bring the console into action. The language used was called Yerkish in honour of Robert M. Yerkes, the distinguished founder of the laboratories for the study of apes that now bear his name.

Orang inhibits chimp

Initially an orang-utan, which had been a companion of Lana for some months, accompanied her in the experimental chamber. It soon became clear that the orang-utan inhibited the chimpanzee's use of the console, and it was removed. Lana asked only for food and drink until she was on her own. Then she would ask for the window to be opened, or would ask to be tickled or groomed by the technician in attendance. Thus, she would depress the overhead bar and press the keys to spell out 'Please Tim groom Lana', or even 'Please Lana groom Tim'. Any sentence was terminated by pressing the period key.

To begin with the chimpanzee was shown how to depress the overhead bar and press the keys, the technician showing her what to do and she imitating his actions. Later, pointing to the correct key was sufficient and eventually verbal guidance including 'Push it', 'Yes', 'No' and 'Finish it', used at a distance was sufficient. Beyond this stage all care was taken to ensure that no cues were given to help Lana formulate her requests or frame her sentences.

Good manners

Only a single key was depressed at first, one which represented M & M candies. Then Lana was required to precede each request with 'Please'. Following this the lexigrams for 'Machine give' and 'M & M' were linked so that one key only needed to be depressed; but the request had to be preceded with 'Please' or no candies appeared.

During the first four months of training Lana became sensitive to errors. When she made one she would press the period key, which erased the images on the projectors, and start again. Gradually her use of 'words' became more flexible, her 'vocabulary' broadened. She had been trained also in the use of 'Yes' and 'No', and there came the time when her technician was drinking a coke in the anteroom. Lana came to the door, her hair erect. She did a foot stomp then went to the keyboard and pressed the key for 'No'.

Conclusions

A study of the many conversations that ensued between Lana and her technicians, and of the varying requests she made not only for food and drink but comfort and recreation, suggests several firm conclusions. First, that the use of a language is linked with intelligence; and that man is facile in language because of his high intelligence. Second, that while chimpanzees do not have the intelligence to generate a language-type communication for themselves they are able to benefit from certain types of human-devized language training programmes. Thirdly, the chimpanzees' facility includes the ability to deal in abstracts such as colours, shapes and spatial movements, and they can do so through various media, such as gestures (sign language), symbols (as in plastic segments) and by visual lexigrams (Yerkish).

Animal tool-users: *efficiency in the world*

The prime tool-user is man, and so he has an unusual interest in seeing how many animals use tools. Until ten to twenty years ago the number of animals known to use tools could be counted on the fingers of one hand. One of the first animal tool-users to be recognized was the digger wasp, the female of which digs shafts in sandy soil. She lays an egg in each shaft, places caterpillars and spiders in the shaft on which the emerging larva can feed, then plugs the shaft with sand. Finally she selects a grain of sand slightly larger than the rest and, holding this in her jaws, taps firm the sand filling the entrance to the shaft.

An Indian elephant uses its trunk as a tool in order to bathe itself with dust

A chimpanzee in a zoo reaches through the bars of its cage. When a chimp was observed using a stick in order to pull into reach food outside its cage, scientists began to investigate other examples of animals and birds using tools

This seems remarkable, that so lowly an animal as an insect should use a tool. Even so, when it was first observed that a chimpanzee in a cage would use a stick to draw within reach of its hand food placed outside the cage, the surprise was even greater. Then scientists began to look for other examples. The male of the Australian bowerbird builds a bower of sticks in which to court the female. In some species he paints the walls of the bower using the juices of coloured berries, applying these with a brush made of a piece of fibrous bark.

Twigs used by many

The woodpecker finch of the Galapagos will probe bark of trees with its bill for insects, but it will also take a cactus spine or a fine twig and, holding it in its bill, drive out insects from crevices. The bird commonly holds the spine or twig in its foot while eating, ready for further probing. This can be compared with the proven habit of chimpanzees of selecting a thin twig or a grass stem, holding it in its mouth while opening up a hole in a termite mound with its finger, then inserting the twig held in its hand. Termites seize the twig in their jaws, it is then withdrawn and passed through the ape's mouth, the termites being chewed from it.

In 1939 E. M. Fisher watched sea otters dive and bring up a mollusk, crab or sea urchin, and also a stone. At the surface the otter would turn on to its back, place the stone on its chest and smash its prey on it to eat the flesh so exposed. At first Fisher's account was treated with scepticism. Now it is well known that sea otters not only use this 'anvil', but will retain the same stone during a number of dives, tucking it in the armpit when both front paws need to be used. A bird that uses an anvil is the European song thrush. It smashes snails on a selected stone to extract the soft body.

Observations in the wild

Tool-using may be defined as the manipulation of an inanimate object with a resulting increase in efficiency in the behaviour pattern of which it is a part. Beginning about the middle of this century there has grown a greater tendency for zoologists to study animals in the wild and increasingly have come further reports of tool-using. Chimpanzees in the wild have been seen to throw sticks to drive away intruders. Female elephants will tear off branches to chastise a disobedient youngster. The orang-utan has been seen to use sticks, as captive chimpanzees will, to reach food and so have several kinds of monkeys.

Deliberate actions

In 1966 came the news that the Egyptian vulture will throw stones at ostrich eggs to break them. It picks up a stone in its beak, raises its head high and throws the stone at the egg with a vigorous movement of head and neck. One vulture was seen to carry a two-pound rock for this purpose and others have been seen carrying stones up to fifty yards to attack an egg. So the action is purposive and deliberate. The most significant aspect of this observation is that it should not have been made before. The Egyptian vulture is found throughout Africa as well as the Middle East and India. Ostriches are not uncommon and formerly were more common. Yet nobody had reported this behaviour until eleven years ago. A few years later it was reported that the Australian black-breasted buzzard-kite breaks open emu eggs by dropping stones on them.

It has happened repeatedly that an item of animal behaviour has been overlooked until recent times, that once attention has been drawn to it reports of it come tumbling in from all quarters. Moreover, it then follows that references to it are found in obscure books. The only conclusion seems to be that people are remarkably unobservant. Take the tool-using of the

Below: one of the first animal tool-users to be recognized was the digger wasp

Below right: a sea otter rests a stone on its chest and uses it as an 'anvil' upon which to crack open a clam

woodpecker finch as an example: this was regarded as unique in birds as late as 1968. Since then nearly twenty species have been observed to use twigs or other inanimate objects. An American robin used a twig to sweep away leaves to uncover insects. A European blackbird used one to sweep an area a foot square of snow nearly two inches thick in its search for food.

Chance observations

All these additional examples have come from chance observations, usually by amateur naturalists, suggesting that tool-using is far more widespread than has been supposed. Thus, a European song thrush, a member of a species that, as has been said, smashes snails on an anvil, was seen to smash snails holding a piece of broken glass in its bill. An elephant was seen to pick up a stick with its trunk to scratch its hide. A water buffalo was seen to pick up a stick in its mouth to scratch itself and a donkey in hot weather, in England, would pick up a sack in its teeth and flick this over its back to drive away flies.

Perhaps most remarkable of all was a moorhen, sitting on her nest, that picked up a piece of polythene lying near by and arranged it over her back when rain began to fall. She carefully tucked in the edges, showing the action was purposive. Moreover, the three observers who watched her for several hours noted that she removed the sheet when the rain stopped and replaced it as the next drops fell, repeating this sequence several times.

Near right: an Egyptian vulture about to try and open ostrich eggs with a stone

Far right: a satin bowerbird building a bower in which to court a female. Bowers are often decorated with berry juice applied with a fibrous bark brush

Below right: a Galapagos tool-using finch probing tree bark for insects with a twig

Below: a great grey shrike uses a spiked twig to secure its prey

Bluebird: *protection of a national favourite*

The eastern or common bluebird, one of three species of bluebird, has long had a special place in the affections of people living in North America, beginning in colonial times. It was welcomed by the early settlers in Plymouth Colony for its friendly behaviour and cheerful song, which reminded them of the robin they had known in the land they left behind them. They named it the blue robin. The bird is also a migrant, breeding in southeastern Canada and the northern states of the United States and migrating to the southern states and Mexico, as far south as Guatemala and Nicaragua for the winter. This reinforced its position as a national favourite for, to many, it became a harbinger of spring.

Symbiotic with man

Like the robin of Europe, with which it was originally compared, it readily accepted the presence of people and their houses, and it used their gardens as a habitat. That is, it became symbiotic with man, one of his good neighbours, with the added virtue that it fed on insects, especially those of the noxious category, including cutworms. Later in the year it turns to wild berries: and at no time does it harm his crops or become a nuisance in any way. Like the European robin it is widespread throughout its range, which comprises the eastern two-thirds of the United States.

When, therefore, the numbers of the common bluebird began to dwindle the fact soon became apparent to all and sundry, especially when the reduction in numbers reached something like ninety per cent. The bluebird is especially susceptible to sudden cold spells and at times these have proved catastrophic, thousands being killed in short spaces of time. A particularly disastrous winter and it may take the survivors five years to pick up again.

It was, however, not the weather that caused the calamitous decline in this revered songster during this century. The first blow was dealt by the bluebird's closest friends, its human neighbours who, with tidy minds, cut down old trees with hollow cavities and replaced old wooden fence posts with neater, more durable metal posts. The bluebird makes its nest in

Even though it is so well loved the bluebird has been victim of man's thoughtless tidying-up of the habitat

Bluebird trails have been established in many parts of the United States in order to protect the threatened bird

suitable holes and hollows, a nest of grasses or pine needles lined with finer grasses or horsehair. In city and country suitable nesting sites became rarer as the human environment became tidier.

Man also dealt the second blow at his favourite bluebird when, with the best intentions, he imported the house sparrow and the starling from Europe. Both are efficient colonists and both have become established and have flourished in the many parts of the world into which they have been introduced. The two also share the habit of nesting in hollows, in trees, buildings and nest-boxes, and are notorious for evicting other birds with this same preference. Both also tend to be symbiotic with man. As the two alien species increased in numbers and spread, the bluebird was driven into open country, apple orchards, open woodlands and country roadsides, harried literally from pillar to post.

Bluebird trails

The modern cult of tree surgery linked with de-forestation has borne heavily on several hole-nesting species. For the bluebird's predicament there was a simple if laborious remedy and bluebird trails have been set up consisting of numbers of nesting-boxes, each box a hundred yards from the next. The boxes need to be cleaned out in the non-breeding season. At all times watch must be kept to oust piratical house sparrows. Starlings can be kept out simply by making the entrance hole precisely one and a half inches. The much larger starling cannot enter.

Dramatic increase

This is a practical essay in conservation and east of the Mississippi river numerous bluebird trails have been set up and more are being laid each year. The numbers of bluebirds have increased dramatically along the trails, which have been described by Dr George E. Watson, curator of birds at the Smithsonian Institution, as 'a network of hope across our great continent'. It will take time to restore the bluebird to its former abundance, but the trail has been blazed. The longest trail, through Canada's Manitoba and Saskatchewan, measures, with its branches, 2000 miles, with more than 7000 nesting-boxes.

Sociobiology: *a new subject*

There used to be a big difference between biology and natural history. Biology was a science, the work of erudite people working in laboratories. Natural history was the observation, in a rather random fashion perhaps, of the daily lives of wild animals and was not usually undertaken by professional scientists. The scientist's criticism of natural history was that it was unorganized and uncritical, but there has been a revolution.

Biology has spilled over from the laboratory into the field. Instead of collecting animals and plants and carrying them indoors, the biologist is increasingly taking his apparatus and notebooks into the countryside to study animals and plants with as little disturbance as possible. One result is that there is an accumulating mass of knowledge about the lives of animals. Detailed analysis has been made of the ways that they find food, avoid enemies, attract mates and rear families, and above all how animal society is organized—whether a species is solitary, territorial or sociable.

Field study

Biologists are largely concerned with evolution and adaptation. In the laboratory they seek, for instance, to understand how a hunting animal has evolved the weapons, in the form of teeth and claws, for catching other animals and how these are adapted for seizing prey. But hunting behaviour has also to evolve and this must be studied in the field. The lion's behaviour is suited for stalking and catching zebra on the African grasslands. Each species has its own unique way of organizing its life and sociobiology is the study of how the social behaviour of animals has evolved and adapted to particular ways of life in various environments. It seeks to draw together the results from field observations and to discover the basic principles underlying the social lives of animals. What is the size of the group in which the animal lives? A large herd, a small family unit or solitary individuals? And how are the chores of food-finding, rearing the family and keeping guard divided among the group? Lions live in a pride and hunt together, while leopards are solitary and hunt alone. According

Above: a flock of North
American icterids arriving at
a reedbed roost at dusk

Left: hunting dogs playing at
Serengeti. Dubbed as 'super
beasts of prey', these dogs are
the most highly socialized of the
canids and known for their
quality of co-operativeness.
They hunt in packs and are
extremely efficient at capturing
prey larger than themselves

to the tenets of evolutionary biology each must have moulded its life style
through natural selection to fit a particular environment.

New perspectives on the hyaena

The relationship of social organization and feeding habits is well shown
by the hyaena family. Once despised as scavengers and parasites living on
other predators' kills, hyaenas are now known also to be active and efficient
hunters in their own right. The brown and striped hyaenas both scavenge
and hunt small animals such as rodents and insects. They lead a solitary
existence, with individuals occupying large territories. The spotted
hyaena feeds on either small antelope, in which case individuals hunt
alone, or on large antelope, when they hunt in groups. Social organization
even varies within a species, which makes it very hard to give a simple
account of its natural history. Such flexibility is shown by a solitary wolf
hunting mice while a wolf pack hunts moose. The reason for this is clear:
an animal can hunt small prey by itself, but needs the co-operation of its
fellows to hunt large prey.

Feeding on large prey is not the only criterion for living communally.
There is safety in numbers and a group of animals can keep a better watch
for enemies and band together to present a united defence. Prairie dogs
feeding on grassland post sentries whose bark of alarm sends the whole
colony rushing to safety. Musk-oxen huddle together, horns outwards, as

a defence against wolves. If prey is well hidden or patchily distributed, a group of animals may have more success in finding it. Flocks of chickadees forage among twigs and foliage and each keeps a watch on the others to see which are the best places to search for insects. Starlings roost in huge flocks and when they set off in the morning, those which have not fed well on the previous day follow those which are returning to a good feeding ground searching for more food.

Overall pattern emerging

Now that there is an overall pattern beginning to emerge from the study of animal social organizations, it is not surprising that some zoologists are speculating how man fits in. Since human beings have been capable of conscious thought, they have asked 'Where have I come from?'. Every race has had myths to account for the origin of man, but it was Darwin who laid firm foundations for the belief that we are descended from animals, our nearest relatives being the chimpanzee and gorilla. Darwin's ideas were vigorously attacked by people who could not accept any physical relationship between man and animals, but we have so many physical attributes linking us to the great apes that there are few people who still deny the relationship.

Behavioural links

The question now being asked is whether our social behaviour is also descended from that of animals and whether there is a biological basis even for such human qualities as aesthetics, religion and ethics. Physically, we

A troop of chacma baboons include one or more dominant males and several subordinate males as well as females and young

are like the great apes, but have developed an upright stance, modified teeth and jaws and, above all, a huge brain. Sociobiologists look to see if there are behavioural links with the great apes upon which specifically human characters have been added, again linked to that huge brain which allows speech and conscious thought. Once again, there is vigorous opposition to the idea of a link between the social behaviour of man and animals. Darwin's ideas of physical evolution were attacked on religious grounds, but sociobiology is attacked for political reasons. Arguments that our social codes and beliefs are inherited could be used, it is suggested, to bolster repressive societies.

Social life

At first sight human and animal social life seem to have little in common, apart from essentials. Human societies, as revealed by sociological studies, seem too far removed from the lives of animals to bear any relation. Some authorities say that the evolution of human societies is wholly different from those of animals. Animal societies evolve through the process of natural selection, with the unfit being weeded out leaving the fit to reproduce their kind. Human societies, on the other hand, evolve by culture. One generation learns from another by experience and teaching. Yet human culture has lasted for only 10,000 years. Before this time, and for the major time in which our species has existed, culture has played only a small part and human evolution was dominated by natural selection. It is therefore very likely, the sociobiologists argue, that truly biological

Chacma baboons engaged in social grooming—an important social activity for all baboons and many primates

A sentry prairie dog sits alert and ready to warn the rest of the colony of potential predators. When defending the territory the dog will give a low bark, which is sometimes accompanied by tooth-chattering if the threat seems to be serious

genetically inherited traits remain in human social behaviour; although these are overshadowed by cultural features. Opponents deny that there is any inheritance of social behaviour; for instance, that the dominance of men over women in so many human societies is a cultural phenomenon with no biological basis or function.

Heated arguments have developed in this discussion of the merits of nature versus nurture in human social evolution and the situation is unlikely to be resolved easily. The problem is that there is no record of how primitive people lived, not only before the advent of historical records, but before human beings left any archaeological record of their doings. The physical evolution of man is based on a few fossil finds and some speculation. Discussion of cultural evolution has to be wholly speculative and it is very dangerous to argue without concrete facts for support. Hopefully, more light will eventually be shed on our ancestry and the intriguing questions of our origin will be answered. Opponents of sociobiology are worried that arguments for social behaviour being inherited from our past can be used to perpetuate injustices such as masculine domination and class structure in modern society. A more optimistic view is to hope that finding the cause for such injustices will also reveal a cure. Taking an analogy from medicine, the discovery that a deranged pancreas causes diabetes led to a cure. It did not result in diabetes being considered an inevitable part of human life.

Alaska pipeline: *disruption of the wildlife*

Alaska has an area of 586,400 square miles. This is about one-sixth of the area covered by continental United States. In 1960 it had a population of 226,000, one person to every two and a half square miles. The figure has now risen to 404,000, nearly half of them living around Anchorage, the major city. Otherwise everything about Alaska is on the grand scale. It has a longer coastline than the whole of continental United States, the highest mountain, Mount MacKinley, in North America, air temperatures that may fall to $-150°F$ in the fierce winter winds and the largest bears in the world. In recent years it has had the costliest commercial enterprise in history, for Alaska is rich in mineral resources, including oil.

Oil rush

In 1968 oil was discovered at Prudhoe Bay, on the Arctic coast, and this set off a 'rush' unequalled in all time. The oil was discovered by the Atlantic Richfield Company (ARCO), who estimated that there was at least fifteen billion barrels of oil and twenty-six trillion cubic feet of natural gas, this amount of oil being sufficient to supply twelve per cent of the petroleum requirements of the United States for the next twenty years. A year later the State of Alaska auctioned off 450,000 acres of oil-lease land near Prudhoe to major oil companies for a billion dollars. The next step was to decide how to get the oil from A to B, A being Prudhoe Bay, ice-bound for much of each year, B being continental United States, the distance between the two being over two thousand miles, as the crow flies, and considerably more by whichever route the oil was transported.

The oil producers considered several different methods: a fleet of ice-breaking giant tankers and a long sea route, a railroad and a pipeline across Canada. Finally, the decision was taken to build a pipeline across Alaska, from north to south, from Prudhoe Bay to the fishing village of Valdez on the ice-free Prince William Sound in the south.

At Valdez the oil would be transferred to tankers. The pipe would be four feet in diameter and 800 miles long; the cost one billion dollars. To finance the project the major oil producers formed a consortium, the Alyeska Pipeline Service Company. Permission was sought from state and federal agencies for a right of way across their lands and this marked the beginning of the great debate, which was to continue for at least five years and prove the most heated, most acrimonious and most complicated in the annals of conservation.

Scenic grandeur

Although Alaska is one vast wilderness its scenery has an almost unrivalled grandeur. Although its ground is largely treeless, largely barren, permanently frozen (permafrost) except for about two feet of soil at the surface which thaws out in summer, the vegetation includes many unique features and, surprisingly, there is a rich fauna, although some elements of it spend nine months of the year in hibernation. Even in summer the countryside, seen from the air, has a desolate flatness broken occasionally by hills of ice (pingos) or mountains, or it is marked by polygonal areas, where frost forms on the unfrozen soil layer on top of the permafrost. Yet the list of animal inhabitants is a formidable one. The mammals include brown bears, wolves and wolverines, polar bear, bison, moose and caribou, musk-ox, mountain goats and Dall sheep, lynx and ground squirrels. The birds are even more numerous and diverse and include two species of swan, seventeen kinds of ducks, and seven geese, two species of eagle, four buzzards, four falcons and the osprey, cranes, ptarmigan, many sea birds and shore birds, even a hummingbird, the rufous hummingbird, manages to intrude into the southeastern corner of Alaska.

The waters, both fresh and salt, yield a long list of species. There are five kinds of salmon and the river otter in the many rivers, as well as smaller fish. In the sea are seals, walrus and sea otter, several kinds of whales, among them the fin whale, blue whale, humpback, bowhead (Greenland right whale) and North Pacific right whale.

Controversial oil

There is also a wealth of marine fish, including food fish and an abundant marine bottom fauna. Since the episode of the *Torrey Canyon*, the oil tanker wrecked off the English coast in 1967, and the thousands of tons of crude oil spilled from the supertanker *Merula* in the Strait of Magellan in 1974, the mere mention of oil is sufficient to make the toes of any ardent conservationist or environmentalist curl. So the idea of extracting the billions of barrels of crude oil from Prudhoe Bay and transporting it, whether by sea or overland, was bound to touch off heated debate.

This is not the place to enter into discussion of the merits or demerits of the case. Rather it is of interest to examine, with almost Olympian detachment, the conflicting issues in one of the most massive essays in conservation. The ice-bound nature of the waters and approaches around Prudhoe Bay led inevitably to the decision to pipe the 'black gold' overland to the eager markets farther south. Long pipelines for the transit of oil exist elsewhere in the world and none of these has caused a furore. In Alaska, however, the situation is strikingly different.

Scarring and disruption

The proposed route for the pipeline runs across the traditional migration route of thousands of caribou, and caribou cannot be expected to leap twice a year over a continuous four-foot pipe to move from their summer breeding grounds to their winter feeding ground and back. Nor, since the herds have followed a specified route for centuries, even millenia, can they be expected to modify their behaviour to allow for an insuperable obstacle in their path. The scarring of the wilderness by an 800-mile pipeline and the disruption to migrating caribou merely epitomize a much wider problem. If this were all that would be involved there could be little effective opposition to a scheme that involves capitalizing on a tremendous buried treasure. Unfortunately, far more is involved.

The disruption of the caribou can be overcome, and is being overcome, by burying the pipe, where this is practicable, or raising it ten feet above the ground, on iron stilts, where it is not. Ten feet would give sufficient clearance for the caribou and their antlers. The work involved to achieve this, with the ancillaries attendant on it, can be best visualized by a few statistics.

Additional upheaval

For the pipe itself over half a million tons of special pipe, from Japan, needed to be transferred to the site. An army of 23,000 workers, men and women, had to be recruited. People need shelter, so camps have to be built. Labourers need recreation, so at Prudhoe a vast recreational complex, on stilts, was built above the snow. It contains a cinema, games room, gymnasium, sauna and non-stop restaurant, a forty-foot swimming pool, even an arboretum with flower gardens. In any community, primitive or advanced, there is a problem of disposal of waste (litter) and sewage. The more complex the life style the higher the problem mounts. There is also the waste from mechanical works, such as empty drums. From October 1968 to May 1969 270,000 tons of freight were flown in by four-engined

Barren ground caribou gather on a high snow patch to seek relief from flies in August

Hercules, every three hours, round the clock. In addition to airfields, roads had to be built, tens of thousands of tons of earth being flown in for the purpose. In burying the pipeline tens of thousands of tons of gravel have to be shifted in digging the necessary trenches.

In temperate latitudes a familiar spectacle is the building of main highways. Almost overnight, it seems, what was previously a quiet stretch of countryside becomes littered with mountains of earth and gravel and scarred by caterpillar tracks and mammoth tyres of heavy lorries. Everything is devastation, yet by the time the highway is finished, the

Raising the pipe to clear the caribou's magnificent antlers is just one suggestion made to avoid disrupting its habitat

ground levelled on either side, returfed, and trees planted, except for the presence of a broad ribbon of roadway and the multiplicity of guide signs, the countryside is returned to something resembling its former beauty and tranquility—relatively at least. The Arctic tundra cannot be so treated with impunity. It represents a delicate ecosystem which, once disturbed, may take decades, even centuries to regenerate. A heavy lorry, loaded with freight, passing once over a strip of virgin tundra may, by the twin processes of erosion and run-off, result in a creek where once was level ground. The tundra vegetation clings precariously to the thin layer of soil above the permafrost. Plant, and animal, communities survive by delicate adaptations to the harsh conditions. They breed and develop slowly because of the harsh conditions and thereby are especially vulnerable to disturbance.

Apprehension

Over the whole gigantic operation broods Mother Earth, ready to exact reparation. In seeking to avenge the scarring of her bosom by roadworks, erosion and run-off is only part of her armoury. The pipeline crosses four earthquake zones. In 1964, Valdez was devastated when a tidal wave washed over the village and its thousand-odd inhabitants, while a hundred miles away in Anchorage, cracks opened in the earth and engulfed whole houses. How would a puny pipeline stand up to this treatment? And if it does not, what will be the effect of a release of oil on to the tundra? Even in the course of construction of the pipeline there have been slight spills from road vehicles, enough to cause environmentalists shivers of apprehension.

The oil companies, in spite of their need to work against time, to press ahead, have given consideration to these and allied problems. The pipeline, for example, takes a zig-zag line as a first precaution so that it can give to the stresses of earth tremors. The pipe itself is in short sections with valves between them so that if a break occurs adjacent sections can be shut off, so minimizing the amount of oil loss. The joints in the pipeline are continually examined, monitored by X-rays. The oil at source is at a high temperature and friction from its flow through the pipe will ensure that this heat is fairly maintained throughout its transit. Where the pipe is buried this heat would tend to be dissipated through the ground, upsetting the permafrost and producing results that are difficult to forecast. For example, the pipe would sink farther into the ground than was intended, perhaps as much as fifty feet. Such things have been foreseen and precautions taken to insulate or offset the heat from the oil.

Tame wildlife

A feature of wildlife living in areas where people are thin on the ground is that it tends to be tame. Bears, wolves and others, even in the preliminary stages of the setting up of camps have wandered in to pick up food and have been fed by the occupants of the camps. The work force has had to be discouraged, sometimes forcibly so, since this particular impact on certain parts of the indigenous fauna may have unfortunate effects in the long run, to the people or to the animals. Grizzly bears, for example, are best kept at arm's length.

The discussion could be continued interminably. Thus, there is at sea a four-billion dollar seafood industry, where any major spillage of oil could

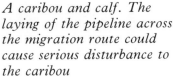

A caribou and calf. The laying of the pipeline across the migration route could cause serious disturbance to the caribou

be disastrous economically and conservation-wise. There are huge deposits of coal in the mountains and already suggestions have been made for open-cast mining. Few things are more calculated to scar beyond repair the virgin beauty of the mountains. Another scheme that could be a major menace is that for building a pipeline to carry the natural gas into Canada. Also, when the highway running parallel to the pipeline is completed this will make travel easier for the transport necessary for the oil working, but would provide easy ingress for the merely curious sightseer and the hunter and sport fisherman. Conservationists envisage parties of hunters disembarking at separate points all along the highway and disappearing into the bush in search of game. With no system of wardens available over such a large area the results, intentional or not, could well be catastrophic to the precarious balance of nature in Alaska.

Unused to the presence of man in the Alaskan wastes, wild animals, such as this polar bear, are usually quite tame and will forage around the camp garbage for food

Lessons and guidance

Already countless millions of words have been written in argument and counter-argument on the problem of the Alaska pipeline. All that can be said has already been said elsewhere, and there is little point in pursuing the subject further here, especially as it could readily lead to partisan argument, which is not our purpose. Perhaps therefore we may conclude with the comment that, in the long term, what is happening in Alaska currently contains materials for study in compromise between economic need and the preservation of the environment and its wildlife. This study could provide valuable lessons and guidance for application on a global scale, and it will be continuous, for the real effects on the environment, and on the vegetation and the animals, of the work so far carried out will not be known for certain for some years ahead.

INDEX

Index

Illustrations

All maps and illustrations by James Marks

Photo credits

Page numbers are in heavy type followed by L (left), R (right), T (top), B (bottom) etc. BC = Bruce Coleman, J = Jacana

2 M. Boulton/BC **4** M. P. L. Fogden/BC **6 L** M. Quraishy/BC **R** R. & M. Borland/BC **7 L** Leonard Lee Rue/BC **R** H. Albrecht/BC **8 L** C. Ott/BC **R** J. Pearson/BC **9 L** M. Price/BC **R** B. Wood/BC **10–11** D. Fossey/BC **13** G. D. Plage/BC **14** Jacana **15** L. Lyon/BC **17 L** Michael Holford **R** Varin Visage/J **18** Bruce Coleman/BC **19** J. P. Varin/J **20** M. P. Price/BC **21 L** M. P. Price/BC **R** M. P. Price/BC **22** M. P. Price/BC **23** M. P. Price/BC **24–5 T** G. D. Plage/BC **B** J. & D. Bartlett/BC **26–7** Charlie Orff/BC **28** Frank Lane **29** M. F. Soper/BC **30** H. Reinhard/BC **31** Bermuda News Bureau & Dept. of Tourism **32 T** P. Johnson/N.H.P.A. **B** Popperfoto **33 T** Alan Hutchinson **B** Australian News & Information Service **34–5** H. Reinhard/BC **36–7** Varin Visage/J **38–9** J. Burton/BC **40–1** C. Zuber/BC **42** N. Myers/BC **43** F. Erize/BC **44** Popperfoto **44–5** Bruce Coleman/BC **46** Popperfoto **47** Popperfoto **48** M. Price/BC **49 L** M. Price/BC **R** M. Price/BC **50–1** M. Price/BC **52** F. Erize/BC **52–3** Bailleau/J **54** Leonard Lee Rue/BC **55** J. & D. Bartlett/BC **56** Varin Visage/J **57** Frank Lane **58** H. Bolton/BC **59** G. D. Plage/BC **60** J. M. Pierce/BC **61** Alan Hutchinson **63** Leonard Lee Rue/BC **64 T** Popperfoto **B** Jacana **66–7** J. Wallis/BC **68** Popperfoto **68–9** Varin Visage/J **70 T** Vogel/Explorer **70–1** R. & M. Borland/BC **72** A. Rainon/J **73** J. Foot/BC **74** F. Erize/BC **75** Sullivan & Rogers/BC **78** Popperfoto **79** C. Zuber/BC **80** M. Price/BC **81** M. Price/BC **82** M. Grant/BC **83** Varin Visage J **84** Popperfoto **85** M. Grant/BC **86** Popperfoto **86–7** Flevet/J **88 T** Varin Visage/J **B** D. & J. Bartlett/BC **88–9** D. Robinson/BC **90** Varin Visage/J **91** J. J. Tullock/BC **92** Popperfoto/UPI **93** A. Rainon/J **94 T** Jeff Goodman **B** P.Nikon/Explorer **95** P.Nikon/Explorer **96–7** J. & D.Bartlett/BC **98** G.D.Plage/BC **99** M.N.Brultan/BC **100** S.C.Bisserot/BC **101** W.Bayer/BC **102** D.Hughes/BC **102–3** D. Hughes/BC **104** J.Burton/BC **105** N.Zuber/BC **106** R.Schroeder/BC **107 L** Mary Evans Picture Library **R** D. & R.Sullivan/BC **108** Brosset/Explorer **109** Popperfoto **110** Australian News & Information Service **111** Australian News & Information Service **113** Dobroutin/Explorer **114 L** Bruce Coleman/BC **R** J.L.S.Dubois/Explorer **115** Varin Visage/J **116 L** Popperfoto **R** C.B.Frith/BC **117** H.Schultz/BC **118** M.Freeman/BC **119** H.Schultz/BC **120** U.Hirsch/BC **120–1** F.Erize/BC **122 L** C.B.Frith/BC **R** E.Gonzales/BC **123** M.P.Harris/BC **124–5** C.B.Frith/BC **125** F.Erize/BC **127** U.Hirsch/BC **128 T** J. & D.Bartlett/BC **B** Frédéric/J **130** J. & D.Bartlett/BC **132** J. & D.Bartlett/BC **133** T.Vogel/Explorer **134–5** R.W.Vaughan/BC **135** J. & D.Bartlett/BC **136** B.Hawkes/J **137** F.Erize/BC **139** Explorer **140** A.Moineau/Explorer **141** B. & J.Dupont/Explorer **142** I.Everson/BC **143** I.Everson/BC **144** I.Everson/BC **145** G.Pizzey/BC **146** Popperfoto **147** Russ Kinne/Photoresearchers Inc. **148** Dr H.E.Dobbs/BC **149** N.Devore/BC **151** United Press International **152** R. & M.Borland/BC **153 L** R. & M.Borland/BC **R** R. & M.Borland/BC **154** N.A.S.A./BC **155 L** I.Everson/BC **R** N.Devore/BC **156 L** Angling Photo Service **R** T.O'Keefe/BC **157 T** G.Langsbury/BC **B** A.Power/BC **158** A.Power/BC **159 T** J.Burton/BC **B** Popperfoto **160–1** H.Reinhard/BC **162** Chris McBride, Timbavati Nature Reserve/Paddington Press **163** M.Grant/BC **164** Popperfoto **165 T** J.Burton/BC **B** Bruce Coleman/BC **167 L** Jeff Goodman **R** Jeff Goodman **169** Yerkes Regional Primate Research Center, Emory University **171** J.Burton/BC **172** C.Zuber/BC **173 L** H.Rivarola/BC **R** J.Foot/BC **174** G.Ziesler/BC **175 TL** J.Pearson **TR** N.Tomlin/BC **B** A.Root/BC **176** Dan Sudia/Photoresearchers Inc. **177** Leonard Lee Rue/BC **178** J.M.Pearson/BC **178–9** M.P.L.Fogden/BC **180** R. & M.Borland/BC **181** R. & M.Borland/BC **182** N.Tomlin/BC **185** C.J.Ott/BC **186** W.E.Ruth/BC **187** S.J.Krasemann/Photoresearchers Inc. **188** J. & D.Bartlett/BC